The Echoes

Living with Cancer

Dr. Larry D. Black

SURVIVORSHIP

The Echoes of Heroes

Living with Cancer

Consider leaving a review of this book to help others find it and grow our community. Thank you for your support.

Contents

FOREWORD

As you read through the following pages, you will embark on a moving and enlightening journey into the lives of individuals who have encountered both the hardships of war and the weight of cancer. This book is the collective voice of their determination, resilience, and sacrifices in the face of adversity. I feel honored to have been allowed to witness and share their stories with the world.

These veterans who have fearlessly served their country on the battlefield are now confronting a new battle — the fight against cancer. Their experiences and struggles shed light on the intricate connections between courage, sacrifice, and the fragility of human life. Through their accounts of triumph over the most challenging situations, we gain a deeper understanding of the often-concealed aspects of being a veteran living with cancer.

As you explore the contents of this book, you will discover stories of veterans who have confronted various difficulties in life but have chosen not to let their health conditions dictate their identity. Everyone has a distinct tale to share, highlighting the tenacity of the human spirit and the influence of companionship.

As you delve into their experiences of overcoming obstacles and achieving success, you will witness the potency of unity, the power of familial connections, and the persistence of the human heart. These narratives are not solely about cancer but also the essence of existence, affection, and the unbreakable bonds that unite us all.

As I have immersed myself in the lives of these extraordinary individuals, I have been deeply touched by their unwavering determination to discover hope amidst hardship, cherish the moments that truly matter, and embrace life with a passion that can only be derived from confronting mortality face-to-face. Their journeys are a powerful reminder that each day is a blessing and that our ability to overcome challenges lies within.

I profoundly hope this book is a tribute — a platform that recognizes and honors these veterans' sacrifices, struggles, and indomitable spirit on their cancer journeys. May their stories inspire us all to value the preciousness of life, unite in moments of adversity, and draw strength from the bonds of empathy and compassion.

As you read through these pages, you're embarking on a voyage of discovery. It may bring tears but also triumph. It may touch wounds but also bring healing. It may open your eyes, and maybe even your heart, to the battles fought silently by those who have already overcome so much while giving so much to the country they love.

If you, a friend, or someone you care about is going through this challenging experience, throw them a lifeline. I highly recommend giving them a copy of **The Echoes of**

Heroes. Along with your prayers and support, this book can help provide hope and inspiration when needed.

Dedication

I honor the memories of the heroic veterans who fought bravely against cancer with all their might. Their unwavering perseverance and fortitude inspired countless individuals to remain resolute in their battle, never surrendering hope and persevering until the end.

Acknowledgments

I want to thank my colleagues who aided me by providing their suggestions, critiques, and encouragement. This book would still be an idea floating around in my head without their support.

I want to thank:

— my wife, Linda, for her love and patience and for allowing me the time and freedom to research and write this book;

— my children, Antoine, Patrick, Brandi, and Terrell, who encouraged me to pursue my dream;

— my good friend, Dr. Dwight Webster, who has been like a brother to me and has helped me when I was down, encouraged me when I was sad, and strengthened me when I was weak;

— Mr. Marcus Clark, Ms. Andrea Henry, and Dr. Joe Grider who provided invaluable guidance and direction;

— Dr. Emmanuel Thompson, for his linguistic and editorial genius because his valuable contributions helped bring this project into reality.

Most of all, I want to thank my God.

INTRODUCTION

A WARRIOR'S PATH

"Today, 50 percent of all cancer patients are being cured of their disease, and another 40 percent go into remission."

—Lois Howland

With the advances in detection and treatment, more people are living with cancer than ever. However, questioning the future and what to expect while fighting the disease is normal.

You may wonder how to navigate this new season of life, from handling fears that your cancer could return to being intimate with another person or whether exercising like you used to is safe. This book intends to help you find support and practical solutions to living with and beyond cancer as you move forward.

These are the poignant tales of true warriors – veterans whose courage, strength, and determination faced the ultimate test when confronted with an enemy far more insidious than any they encountered on enemy shores. (Names changed for privacy)

This narrative unravels the transformative moments, the heartaches, and the triumphs of veterans battling cancer. It delves into the emotional turmoil of facing an uncertain future, grappling with mortality, and navigating the maze of medical interventions.

Through the tears and the smiles, these veterans emerged as an emblem of hope, embodying the resilience they once demonstrated in service to their country.

In this odyssey, these veterans are not just fighting for their survival but also for their comrades who were injured and disabled during battle. Their inspiring journey has given hope to other veterans and cancer patients, showcasing their unwavering determination and solidarity.

Throughout this poignant account, we witness the unwavering support from family, friends, and a grateful nation. We gain insight into the incredible support systems that rallied behind these men and women, reinforcing the profound truth that no warrior ever stands alone.

As we journey alongside these brave souls, we are reminded of the frailty and beauty of life and how adversity can foster remarkable growth. These stories testify to the human spirit's extraordinary capacity to endure, overcome, and emerge from the depths of darkness, more robust and resilient than ever.

Join us as we embark on this courageous expedition – a chronicle of a group of veterans' unwavering will to survive, fight, and inspire. A saga that unveils the true essence of heroism and perseverance in the face of cancer's most formidable challenge. These are their echoes – these warriors living with cancer.

CHAPTER ONE

TESTED BY FIRE

"Time is all you have. And you may find one day that you

have less than you think."

—Randy Pausch

Cancer is a disease that impacts a significant number of individuals across the globe. Receiving a diagnosis can be heartbreaking for people of any age, gender, or ethnic background, even clergy.

Coping with the physical, emotional, and spiritual difficulties that come with the condition can be daunting for patients and their loved ones. The journey from diagnosis to end of life can be long and challenging, as it involves dealing with various emotions and obstacles.

For two decades, Reverend Anderson had selflessly served as a chaplain in the armed forces, bringing comfort, hope, and solace to military members and their families during war and peace.

His unwavering dedication to his calling earned him the respect and admiration of those he served, making him a beloved figure in the community. One fateful day, his life turned unexpectedly when he received a life-altering diagnosis: "It may be cancer."

Reverend Anderson said, "It was a frightening wake-up call when my doctor told me that he saw something on the scan of my esophagus. I heard 'cancer.'

The discovery of a nodule on one of my vocal cords led to shock, numbness, and my worst fears as I thought about the treatment, side effects, test results, and long-term outcome, as well as how a cancer diagnosis would affect my family, ministry, and others.

"As I sat across from my doctor, absorbing the gravity of the news, the sudden and unexpected announcement momentarily paralyzed me, creating an emptiness in my stomach's pit, creating shock and disbelief. Fear, uncertainty, and anger crashed over me. Feeling numb, I thought, 'This can't be true; there must be a mistake since I don't feel sick.'

"For six years, I had walked, prayed, counseled, and provided for Veterans suffering from, living with, and recovering after cancer. I saw, heard, and felt the pain, suffering, sadness, and sorrow, along with the joy and relief of patients and families fighting for their lives.

"As an Oncology Chaplain, I was experienced in addressing the unique spiritual, religious, and emotional needs of individuals with cancer. I had to draw on that experience in my own time of need.

"In my work, I provided daily pastoral care to veterans and their families experiencing spiritual distress, new cancer diagnoses, treatment decision-making processes, changing care goals from curative to palliative, and end-of-life issues.

"I helped veterans search for meaning in their illness and facilitate relationship reconciliation. I offered consultation and counsel on spiritual, emotional, and ethical matters by listening without judgment, sharing without preaching, and providing resources such as tradition, sacraments, scripture, ritual, and personal presence.

"I used spiritual assessments to identify factors contributing to the veteran's stress and suffering. This is how I learned to be attuned to the internal struggles that others around me could not see.

"My pastoral visits brought comfort and reassurance, providing a safe space for veterans to reconnect with their faith and share their deepest fears and concerns, such as the loss of identity, the pain of a diagnosis, and the fear of being abandoned by loved ones or their faith community.

"Those who are battling cancer and their loved ones who may be experiencing spiritual struggles can find comfort and hope through spiritual care. We Chaplains play an important role in this process by creating a nurturing environment that allows patients to explore and address their spiritual needs.

"By offering compassionate spiritual care as part of the patient's treatment plan, chaplains can assist cancer patients in overcoming the challenges they may face during their illness.

"Through open-ended questioning, I created a spiritual care plan that addressed each veteran's unique spiritual needs, focusing on three universal spiritual needs:

- love and connection,

- meaning and purpose,

- and forgiveness.

"By understanding their spirituality, rituals, and practices, I provided support that reaffirmed their values and offered compassionate care.

"I was well versed in the stages of living with cancer from diagnosis to death. Yet, facing this crucible, my possible death sentence, I reacted like everyone else.

"With all my education, training, and experience as a Board-Certified clinically trained Chaplain, with all the support and help I had provided others, I was unprepared and shocked by the announcement of a possibly fatal illness such as cancer.

"After recoiling from the shocking news and discovering myself in the stunning and unnerving situation of having to navigate living while perhaps dying, I knew I had to cope with this new state of uncertainty by accepting its reality and adjusting my lifelong attitude from helping those with cancer to now joining them.

"The threat of serious illness not only unleashed a variety of moods and emotions but also a desire to find answers. I fluctuated between fear and hope, longing and desire, sorrow and joy, and confidence that modern medicine would find a way to help me.

"While waiting for the lab results, despite the fear and worry, I was perplexed and unsettled about 'what if' and coming to terms with my possible cancer diagnosis.

"Receiving a cancer diagnosis was overwhelming and caused much anxiety and worry about various aspects such as pain, physical changes, managing responsibilities, and mortality. After being diagnosed, it's natural to feel scared, but sometimes these emotions are based on rumors, false stories, or inaccurate information. I wanted to be sure I was informed.

"So, I learned as much as possible about my type of cancer. By obtaining factual knowledge, I felt more prepared and less afraid. Educating myself was one way I could take an active role in my care, which improved my commitment to treatment plans that promoted faster recovery.

"Once I came to terms with the possibility of a cancer diagnosis, I went into planning mode. I focused on where to receive the best possible treatment and educated myself about nodules on the vocal cords, including stage, prognosis, necessary tests, and available treatments.

"I also inquired about alternative therapies and weighed the advantages, disadvantages, and risks. I searched for medical knowledge But it wasn't just an intellectual pursuit. I needed to do inner work as well. I reassessed my strengths, weaknesses, spiritual beliefs, and support system.

"Though fear tried to overwhelm me, I was no stranger to adversity. I had walked alongside countless soldiers, sailors, airmen, and marines through their darkest moments, providing strength and hope in times of turmoil. I had been down this road many times as a guide. Now, I might need to be the one who is guided.

"Drawing from my well of faith, I resolved to face my diagnosis with the same courage and determination I had shown throughout my life.

"With my faith as a guiding light, I found solace in prayer, meditation, and guided imagery. I leaned on my relationship with God, finding comfort in knowing I was not alone in my battle against a life-threatening disease.

"Through my vulnerability and honesty, I discovered that sharing my struggles with others strengthened my faith, inspired those around me, and touched lives in new and profound ways.

"Being set afloat on this journey to self-discovery helped me develop a positive mindset, adapt to my situation, and recognize the opportunity I had been gifted with.

"When the lab results confirmed that the nodule was benign, relief washed over me, and I felt the negative, powerful emotions of fear, despair, anger, and guilt fade, and peace of mind envelop me.

"Having experienced what many cancer patients live with, the mindset, understanding, and the emotional stages they progress through, I knew I had received a gift and must change my approach to providing spiritual and emotional support.

"Through my writings, sermons, and interactions, I offer hope and impart wisdom and inspiration to veterans by encouraging them to develop their faith from the lessons I learned during my courageous battle.

"Because veterans, like many in our society, tend to avoid contemplating death, I help them maintain a positive outlook when dealing with a prolonged illness such as cancer. By adopting a positive mindset, approaching life with renewed energy, and finding meaning and purpose in their illness, veterans can grow spiritually and find comfort and commitment during their cancer journey.

"Like a skilled horticulturist, I cultivate the soil of the soul, removing those things that impede growth, and planting seeds of inspiration that encourage new beginnings—things that regrow spiritual and emotional health."

As the rising sun rises at a new dawn, this veteran chaplain courageously ministers to those living with cancer and shines brightly. His life of courage, service, and unwavering faith continues to influence those who know him, his spirit lives on in the hearts of those he touches, and his story continues to inspire generations.

SPIRITUAL SUPPORT

Reverend Anderson's story highlights the power of support — both giving and receiving. Cancer is a complex and often devastating disease that affects the body, mind, emotions, and spirit. Many cancer patients and their families struggle with questions of meaning, purpose, and hope as they face the challenges of diagnosis, treatment, and recovery. Chaplain support can provide comfort, guidance, and spiritual care for cancer patients and their families.

Chaplains are trained professionals who offer spiritual care to veterans, families, and healthcare staff. They come from various faith traditions, but their primary focus is on meeting the spiritual needs of patients and their families, regardless of their religious backgrounds.

They provide a range of services, including prayer, meditation, counseling, and emotional support, and they often work closely with healthcare providers to ensure that patients receive holistic care.

Cancer patients may have a variety of spiritual needs and concerns. Some may struggle with questions of faith and meaning, while others may experience guilt, anger, or despair. Chaplains can help patients explore these issues and find ways to cope.

They may offer spiritual resources, such as prayer or meditation, that patients can use to find comfort and solace. They may also help patients connect with faith-based communities or spiritual leaders who can provide additional spiritual support.

Chaplains can also offer emotional support to cancer patients and their families. They can listen to patients' concerns and offer them a safe and supportive environment where they can express their feelings. They are even trained to talk with patients who are angry, confused, or afraid.

They can provide validation, empathy, and understanding, which can be particularly valuable for patients who feel isolated or misunderstood. And they often help patients navigate complex decisions like end-of-life care or treatment options.

In addition to offering spiritual and emotional support, chaplains can help patients and their families navigate the healthcare system as they advocate for patients, helping them communicate with healthcare providers to meet their needs. They are a rich resource for information about healthcare resources and services and help patients and their families understand their options and make informed decisions.

Chaplain support can be precious for cancer patients facing the end of life. They help patients find meaning and purpose in their lives, even in the face of illness or other challenges. They might help patients connect with faith-based communities or spiritual leaders who can provide additional spiritual support.

Chaplain support is an essential component of cancer care. They provide spiritual, emotional, and practical support to patients and their families, helping them cope with cancer diagnosis, treatment, and recovery challenges.

By offering spiritual care and resources, chaplains help patients find meaning, hope, and comfort during difficult times and can improve their overall quality of care.

CHAPTER TWO

UNWAVERING FAITH

"The diagnosis of cancer is not an automatic death warrant

that demands the patient and their family stop living."

—*Stephanie Matthews Simonton*

In the face of life's most daunting challenges, faith has often served as a beacon of hope and strength for individuals. One such example is the inspiring journey of Jasmine, a Christian woman who, when confronted with the harrowing battle against cancer, embraced her faith as a powerful weapon to overcome adversity.

With unwavering conviction, she turned to her beliefs, drawing upon the teachings of Christianity to navigate the tumultuous waters of her illness. This story delves into the profound impact of her faith, highlighting how it provided solace, resilience, and a deep sense of purpose throughout her battle with cancer.

It also shows how her incredible faith strengthened her to ask God to use her as his chosen vessel even before the official diagnosis.

"I was diagnosed with invasive ductal carcinoma of the left breast at 49. So, I started chemotherapy, the only option to treat HER2-positive breast cancer. I also underwent a bilateral mastectomy.

"Post-surgery pathology showed a small residual disease, so I started on prescription medicine to treat HER2-positive breast cancer to destroy any detected cancer cells and reduce the recurrence risk.

"Receiving a cancer diagnosis was a very overwhelming experience that stirred up various emotions. I felt frightened, nervous, optimistic, comforted, saddened, and relieved as I processed that while medical treatments could aid in battling illness, there were no certainties of a positive outcome.

"Once I recovered from the shock and accepted the truth, I turned to the ONE I knew could manage my circumstances and restore my hope for the future."

"Fear and uncertainty tried to cloud my mind during this diagnosis of cancer. However, my faith offered a sanctuary of solace and comfort. I sought refuge in prayer and journaling, pouring my heart out to God, sharing my deepest fears, and seeking strength to face each day. I wrote about my feelings, thoughts, and spiritual insights to gain clarity and perspective.

"My intimate connection with the divine gave me a sense of peace, knowing I was never alone in my struggle. It was a constant reminder that a Higher Power was watching over me, guiding my steps and offering support in my darkest moments.

"Christianity emphasizes the importance of community and fellowship. Drawing on this biblical principle, I sought support from family, friends, and my church community. Prayers, encouragement, and unwavering support from loved ones and fellow believers became a source of strength throughout my cancer journey.

"They rallied around me, offering words of comfort, accompanying me to medical appointments, and uplifting my spirits during the most challenging times. My Christian community became a tangible expression of God's love, encouraging me to persevere.

"Central to Christian theology is the belief that God has a plan for every individual's life. I found immense strength in surrendering to this divine plan, trusting that there was a greater purpose at work, even during my illness.

"I freed myself from the burdensome weight of anxiety and uncertainty by relinquishing control and trusting God. This unwavering trust allowed me to face each treatment, setback, and obstacle with courage, knowing that, ultimately, God was orchestrating my healing journey.

"Cancer is a formidable adversary that tests one's resilience and endurance. However, I drew upon my faith that taught me that God is the source of limitless strength. I could overcome any obstacle through Him.

"In moments of physical weakness, doubt, or pain, I clung to the promises of scripture, finding encouragement in verses such as Philippians 4:13, which states, "I can do all things through Christ who strengthens me." This unwavering belief fueled my determination to fight cancer with all my might.

"Rather than succumbing to despair, I viewed my battle with cancer as an opportunity to be an instrument of hope and inspiration for others. My faith instilled a deep sense of purpose, compelling me to share my resilience, faith, and healing story with those around me.

"Through my testimony, I seek to uplift others facing similar trials, reminding them that they are not alone and that there is always hope in God. My unwavering faith became a beacon of light in the darkness, inspiring others to find strength in their spiritual journeys.

"It took me a whole year to fight the cancer in my body, and I'm happy to say I won that fight. Years later, I'm still doing fine. Better than fine. Yes, I deal with grief, pain, and fear daily. But for all that cancer took away from me, it gave me something extraordinary.

"Cancer gave me a new perspective on life, allowing me to live my life in the moment, with intention. Cancer reminded me that life is short and that tomorrow is not promised. I often hear people ask, "Where has the time gone?" Not me. "I can honestly account for every minute of every day since my diagnosis. I don't take one moment for granted. I don't sweat the small stuff. I don't back down from a challenge. And I savor each moment with the people I love—cancer did that, and for that, I am grateful."

FAITH

The story of Jasmine's battle with cancer showcases the transformative power of faith. She found solace, support, resilience, and purpose through her unwavering conviction of God's providence. Her faith in God allowed her to face the formidable challenge of cancer with courage, knowing that she was never alone.

Her journey is a powerful testament to the profound impact that faith can have in navigating life's most challenging circumstances. Jasmine's unwavering faith became a powerful force when used to combat cancer and inspire those around her.

Being diagnosed with cancer can cause a range of emotions for veterans and their loved ones, such as shock, fear, anger, and sadness. It can be overwhelming to come to terms with the fact that their lives will be permanently altered and they will have to navigate medical appointments, treatments, and decisions.

As the illness progresses, veterans may experience physical symptoms like pain, fatigue, nausea, and emotional challenges such as depression, anxiety, and grief. Coping with these difficulties requires a strong support system that includes family, friends, and healthcare providers who can offer comfort and care.

A cancer diagnosis is challenging for anyone, leading to emotional turmoil for the patient and their loved ones. Coping with the possibility of death and the accompanying emotional distress can be difficult, but taking steps to reframe our outlook and find inner peace is essential.

To prevent feeling lost and overburdened, we must confront and accept the situation and seek support from our loved ones and healthcare providers.

While receiving a cancer diagnosis can cause intense feelings of fear, despair, and anger, they may eventually diminish. However, living with a chronic and possibly fatal illness can lead to accumulating anxiety.

Balancing emotions and integrating them into daily life is crucial without losing focus is a full-time job for those living with cancer. Despite this emotional rollercoaster, it's essential to persist in seeking the truth of each situation.

It's also important to recognize that physical, emotional, financial, and social obstacles may arise, even if your condition has been cured or is in remission. Overcoming challenges like denied insurance claims, workplace discrimination, and building a support system is crucial.

It's important to stay independent and prevent any anxieties about your illness from taking over your life. Staying focused can help make your life more fulfilling and productive.

During this critical period of illness, it's vital to make necessary medical decisions, such as selecting a qualified doctor to oversee treatment and guided you to make appropriate choices. Even if issues such as uncertain lab results or X-ray reports undermine your confidence, it's vital to remain positive and tackle new challenges calmly to discover solutions.

Many veterans diagnosed with cancer turn to their spiritual values and religious beliefs to cope with their illness and find a deeper meaning to their lives and the reason for their sickness. For many, their belief in God is integral to their spiritual journey.

While cultural and religious traditions may shape their spiritual needs, most veterans and their caregivers rely on their faith for comfort and support throughout their cancer journey.

Some religious individuals may turn to pastoral care to connect with a Higher Power when seeking meaning and purpose. However, they may question why they are suffering with their illness when faced with a cancer diagnosis and struggle to reconcile their beliefs.

During these difficult times, religion can offer comfort and reassurance. The Book of Psalms can provide much-needed emotional support, with the Psalmist empathizing and offering comfort during times of crisis.

The 23rd Psalm is especially well-known and reads, *"Yea though I walk through the valley of the shadow of death, I will fear no evil, for thou are with me; your rod and your staff, they comfort me."* (KJV)

When dealing with cancer or other serious illnesses, we may become more aware of the beauty and harshness of life, intensifying our emotions and deepening our connection with the world.

Simplifying our lives and dedicating ourselves to others through asceticism is a common practice in religious history. Religion teaches us that certain practices can enhance our spiritual well-being and energy, giving us direction and order.

Religious teachings have long acknowledged the experience of facing death and adversity and have drawn on the stories of wise people who have walked this path before us. These stories can guide us and provide insight into our journey. Ultimately, our emotions can lead us to a deeper understanding of the world and a closer relationship with God.

Cancer patients may struggle to manage their daily lives as their usual routines may no longer be appropriate. Religious teachings can guide us in how to behave according to our values. Additionally, structured practices from various spiritual traditions can offer further guidance.

Religious practices, such as prayer, healing practices, meditation, guided meditation, and anointing, can provide comfort, support, and guidance for cancer patients. These practices allow us to express our pain, joy, grief, loneliness, and isolation while tapping into our emotions.

Prayer can provide comfort in various ways, such as solace, encouragement, and connection. It can also bring a sense of power and mystery, allowing us to feel the presence of divinity and love as we pray.

In modern times, healing practices related to religion have become increasingly prevalent. Many people seek spiritual healing and comfort through religious traditions and practices, recognizing the value of healing prayer services and rituals and more conventional prayers and rituals.

Religious resources and practices can provide helpful coping mechanisms when dealing with cancer. Clergy members can be an excellent source of support, comfort, and guidance during difficult times.

It's important not to overlook the significant value of clergy visits in helping people cope with cancer. Their presence conveys a powerful message about God's care for the ill, representing tangible evidence of God's caring presence.

CHAPTER THREE

VICTORIOUS OVER THE ADVERSARY

"You can be a victim of cancer or a survivor of cancer. It's a mindset."

Dave Pelzer

Don G, a proud Marine veteran, spent his younger years serving his country with unwavering dedication and courage. Throughout his military career, he faced countless battles on the front lines and behind the scenes. However, little did he know that his most formidable adversary was yet to come—a battle with cancer.

"I always cared for my health, going for regular check-ups and leading an active lifestyle. But in my early seventies, I started experiencing unusual symptoms. Persistent fatigue, discomfort on my left side, and occasional lower back pain troubled me. Concerned, I scheduled an appointment with my doctor, hoping for reassurance.

"She sent me for a CT scan, which came back with liver cancer. I was a veteran and went to the C. W. Bill Young VA Medical Center in Bay Pines, Florida. They conducted some tests and sent me for a liver biopsy and PET scan.

"Following this series of tests and examinations, I received the unexpected news—my cancer had migrated from my liver to my esophagus, and I had a 10 cm tumor in my stomach. The diagnosis hit me like an enemy ambush. I was stunned, overwhelmed, scared, and angry.

"My heart started pounding in my chest, and I went numb. A suffocating sensation and panic overcame me, and I felt a mixture of fear, uncertainty, and determination to fight this battle head-on, just as I had throughout my military service.

"With the support of my loving wife and children, I set out on my journey to conquer cancer. The battle would be challenging, but I was ready to face it with the same resilience and bravery that had defined my military career.

"I consulted with the oncology doctor at the VA Medical Center, and they sent me to see a team of expert doctors and specialists at the Florida Cancer Center who would guide me through my treatment.

"During my initial consultation with them on June 13th, 2022, I was told I had metastatic cancer and 18 months to live. Upon hearing this diagnosis that I didn't have a chance, I became outraged, shouting, 'I will beat cancer,' and walking out of the doctor's office.

"The next day, my wife and I headed to the Bay Pines VA Medical Center, feeling very emotional, where we met the Oncology Supervisor, Senada, who took me by the hand and set up my port and oncology appointments.

"She recommended combining therapies, including surgery, radiation, and hormone therapy. Fully aware of the risks and potential side effects, I understood that every decision would require careful consideration. As a Marine, I went into "Deal with it mode" and ensured we educated ourselves and developed a plan.

"The oncology team agreed that they would have to shrink the tumor, so I underwent very aggressive chemotherapy to shrink the tumor. I received two very aggressive rounds of chemotherapy every day for five weeks. During treatment, I experienced a rollercoaster of emotions.

"There were moments of physical and emotional pain when I doubted my strength and questioned if I could endure the relentless assault on my body. But I refused to let despair consume me, drawing inspiration from my fellow veterans who had faced their own battles with courage and resilience.

"I found solace in connecting with other cancer veterans during my treatment. I joined the weekly virtual cancer support group where I discovered a network of individuals who understood my struggles and offered invaluable guidance.

"These connections, built on shared experiences and unwavering support, helped me regain my hope and purpose. As time passed, my determination began to yield results.

"The cancer started to retreat, slowly but surely, under the relentless barrage of treatments. Each small victory further fueled my resolve, pushing me forward with an indomitable spirit.

"Months came and went, and with each passing day, I grew more robust. My perseverance and the unwavering support of my wife, family, and friends never wavered. We celebrated the milestones together, whether it was a successful surgery, the completion of a round of radiation, or positive news from a follow-up appointment.

"My great wife kept working, changed all her schedules, cooked my new cancer meals, and picked me up from the ground when chemo kicked my butt.

"Throughout my journey, I learned the true meaning of resilience and the power of a united front. Just as I had relied on my comrades on the battlefield, I leaned on my loved ones for strength, support, and encouragement.

"Their unwavering belief in my ability to overcome every obstacle was the bedrock upon which I built my victory. Throughout my process, the level of care was just outstanding. It was comforting to know that I was receiving the best care possible.

"Finally, after months of tenacious battles, the cancer was in remission. I and the wife emerged triumphant, crying when my doctors told me I had beat stage four cancer and declared me cancer-free, a testament to my courage and the incredible advances in medical science.

"The scars of the fight remain — physical and emotional — but they are reminders of my resilience and the battle I have conquered. My wife told me every day that we would beat this together. We did! God's grace led me to my guardian angels at the Bay Pines VA Medical Center."

With his cancer battle behind him, Don dedicated himself to raising awareness about the disease, supporting fellow survivors, and advocating for improved healthcare for veterans. He knew that his fight was not in vain and that his experience could make a difference in the lives of others facing similar battles.

He says, "I beat cancer with God's hands, prayers, and determination. I believe it's the attitude inside and the desire to live that allowed me to beat this disease, and if it comes back, by the grace of God, I will beat it again.

Unfortunately for me, life had another cruel twist as the cancer returned, this time with even greater ferocity. Upon hearing the news, the room grew silent, my heart started racing, and I felt the numbness returning and the suffocating anxiety building again.

"It seemed as if the world was testing my resolve, challenging me to face an adversary that had already brought me to my knees once before.

"But I am not one to back down. I took several deep breaths to calm my heart and focused on positive images to reduce my anxiety. I refuse to let cancer define me or determine my fate. So, after a second diagnosis, I felt hope despite the difficult news.

"Once again, I embarked on the arduous journey of treatments and surgeries, enduring the physical and emotional toll they exacted. Each day, I grew stronger, determined to overcome this insidious disease.

"Finally, after countless trials and tribulations, the day arrived when I received the news I had longed to hear. I had beaten cancer for the second time. The battle had been fierce, leaving scars both seen and unseen, but I emerged triumphant, my spirit shining brighter than ever.

"After two rounds of cancer, my most significant adjustment is the constant fear of cancer returning. 'It's a nagging feeling that's always there. In my joy, when I'm happy, even when I have a new ache or pain, it's always accompanied by 'What if?'"

Though he had fought many battles, Don G, the Marine veteran turned cancer survivor, proved that fighting for one's life is the most crucial battle. And he fights it with the same courage, resilience, and honor that had defined his military career holding on to hope in the face of uncertainty.

<u>HOPE</u>

Millions of individuals who have had cancer are still alive today, and there are better chances of living with and beyond cancer than ever before. Cancer patients can continue to lead active lives during treatment as well.

Some doctors believe that having a hopeful outlook and positive attitude can aid in dealing with cancer; written studies support this. To build hope, plan your days as usual, and do not limit yourself because of cancer.

You can also look for reasons to be hopeful, writing them down or talking to others about them to understand your thoughts more clearly. Spending time in nature, reflecting on spiritual beliefs, and listening to stories about active cancer survivors can also help.

Cancer is a complex condition that affects people differently and can significantly impact their physical, emotional, and social well-being. The experience will vary greatly depending on the category and stage of cancer and the individual's overall health and support system.

Following a cancer diagnosis, the first step is developing a treatment plan. Using a multidisciplinary approach this includes medical care, emotional and psychological support, and lifestyle changes.

This plan may also involve surgery, radiation therapy, chemotherapy, targeted therapy, or a combination of these approaches. The treatment plan will depend on various aspects, such as the category and stage of cancer, the person's overall health, and preferences.

Many people experience physical and emotional side effects during treatment, including fatigue, pain, nausea, depression, and anxiety. The best strategy is to communicate openly with their healthcare teams about any symptoms they are experiencing, as there are often ways to manage or alleviate these side effects.

As treatment progresses, the healthcare team will monitor the person's response to treatment and adjust the plan as needed. For some people, treatment successfully eradicates or puts the cancer into remission. For others, the tumor may continue to progress despite treatment.

Cancer may sometimes become advanced or metastatic, meaning it has spread to other areas in the body. At this point, the focus of treatment may shift to palliative care, which aims to manage symptoms and improve quality of life. Palliative care may include pain management, emotional support, and assistance with daily activities.

For some people with advanced cancer, hospice care may be appropriate. Hospice care provides comprehensive support for individuals in the final stages of life, focusing on comfort and quality of life. Hospice care may occur in a specialized facility or the person's home, depending on their preferences and needs.

While a cancer diagnosis can be overwhelming, it is essential to remember that many resources and support systems are available to help individuals navigate their journey and manage their symptoms. Cancer survivors need a robust support system, including healthcare providers, family, friends, and support groups.

Open communication, self-care, and maintaining a sense of hope and purpose can also help cope with the challenges of cancer. With the proper support, many people with cancer can maintain a high quality of life and continue to pursue their goals and interests.

People diagnosed with chronic and potentially fatal diseases like cancer often exhibit similar patterns of reactions, thoughts, and behaviors. However, it is essential to note that not everyone will experience all these actions. Some may experience more than others. Knowing and understanding these emotions can help us confront our uncertainties and make informed decisions.

It's important to acknowledge the emotional impact of a long-term illness that may have periods of remission and that offers chances for recovery. The rollercoaster effect can be daunting. While healthcare professionals focus on physical health, we should prioritize our emotional well-being to be able to ride the waves as they come.

Loved ones can offer valuable support to help us navigate this challenging time. With their help, we can regain confidence, cope with fear and anxiety, discover new sources of meaning and fulfillment, experience satisfaction, and ultimately achieve peace of mind.

Everyone has unique preferences, so no single approach to life works for everyone. Some people need a detailed, step-by-step breakdown with lists of options and ideas, while others only need minimal guidance from their healthcare provider.

Some individuals may find comfort in their religious beliefs and make faith in God a cornerstone of their existence, while others may benefit from the support of their loved ones and social groups. The important thing is to implement what works best for you.

Humans tend to associate positive outcomes with our actions and adverse effects with mistakes. When disasters, like collapsed construction sites or power plant explosions, occur, it is vital to conduct a thorough investigation to identify the cause and hold those responsible accountable.

Similarly, when we fall ill, it's a psychological response to guilt to blame ourselves and deserve punishment rather than accepting that illness is not always within our control.

Sometimes, people experience survivor's guilt, which means they feel unworthy of their good fortune when others have suffered or died. They may worry that they'll be punished for surviving and lose confidence.

But it's important to remember that surviving a tragedy doesn't mean they caused harm to others. To overcome negative emotions, it's essential to focus on moving forward.

For some people, attending group therapy sessions in a comfortable setting can also effectively relieve psychological stress. It's important to remember that these methods may not eliminate anxiety.

Still, they can provide an outlet for intense emotions such as fear, anger, and guilt that may arise during a life-threatening illness. The first step towards managing negative emotions during this phase of confronting mortality is acknowledging them.

CHAPTER FOUR

A JOURNEY OF COURAGE AND GRACE

"We must be willing to get rid of the life we've planned,

so as to have the life that is waiting for us."

—Joseph Campbell

The battle against cancer is an arduous and deeply personal journey that tests the strength, resilience, and spirit of patients and their loved ones. Within this struggle lie stories of profound bravery, love, and the triumph of the human spirit.

This story recounts the powerful narrative of a veteran's courageous battle with cancer, highlighting their unwavering determination, the support they received, and the legacy they left behind.

Our story begins with the life-altering moment when a 72-year-old Navy veteran, Charlie C, was diagnosed with colorectal cancer, which changed everything. The shock and uncertainty that followed became the backdrop of his new reality.

"My gaze fixed on the doctor's somber expression, absorbing every word as if I were on the front lines again, awaiting orders."

'I'm sorry to tell you, Charlie, but the biopsy results confirm that you have cancer,' the doctor said gently, her voice filled with empathy.

"When the doctor delivered the news, the room fell silent, and time seemed to stand still. I am a seasoned veteran who has faced battles on distant shores and seen my fair share of hardships. I momentarily felt detached, as if watching the scene outside my body.

"Then, reality crashed over me like a tidal wave, and I felt the weight of those words deep within my soul. Memories of comrades lost in the line of duty, and the trials of war flooded my mind, but this enemy, this battle, was one I had never expected to face.

"My eyes welled with tears, threatening to spill over. I tried to maintain the composure that had served me well throughout my military career, but this diagnosis was unlike anything I had ever experienced. It was a vulnerability I had never allowed myself to show, even during the darkest days of combat.

"I met with my new doctor: an oncologist. The doctor's empathetic gaze softened as she handed me a box of tissues, allowing me a moment to collect my emotions. She knew that even the bravest sailors had their breaking points, and this was undoubtedly one of mine.

"As I wiped away the tears that had escaped, I mustered the strength to speak, my voice shaky but determined. 'How bad is it? What's the prognosis?' I asked, trying to gain some semblance of control over the situation.

"The doctor explained the severity of the cancer, detailing the treatment options and the uncertainties ahead. I absorbed every word, recognizing the gravity of the situation. It wasn't about fear of my mortality; after all, death had danced around me in war, inching closer countless times. It was the realization that this battle was not fought with weapons and comrades at my side but within the confines of my own body.

"Thoughts of family flooded my mind—the wife who had been my anchor throughout my military service, the children I had watched grow up while I was away, and the grandchildren I hoped to see one day.

"I didn't want them to see me in this vulnerable state, but I knew I had to confront this illness head-on, just as I had done with every challenge in the past. Questions arose, fears consumed, and a flicker of hope emerged. Armed with determination, I resolved to face the battle head-on, determined to find strength amidst the storm.

"As I left the doctor's office, I couldn't shake the emotional weight that now burdened me. I thought about the camaraderie I had experienced with my fellow sailors, the deep bond formed through shared hardship and sacrifice. I realized that, once again, I needed a support network, this time to face the fight against cancer.

"In the following days, I attended appointments, treatments, and therapy sessions, surrounded by the unwavering support of my loved ones and fellow veterans. I became active in my care by educating myself about my specific type of cancer to feel more empowered.

"I dedicated ample time to researching my type of cancer on the computer. As a planner, I realized I needed to alter my approach to life. Instead of focusing on living year to year, I now focus on how to spend the time between treatments.

"There were difficult moments when I questioned if I had enough fight left in me, but each time I wavered, the memory of my comrades and the unwavering spirit of the military community spurred me on.

"As I embarked on this new battlefield, I learned that sometimes the bravest thing a sailor can do is face the enemy on the front lines and confront the vulnerability and emotions within.

"And so, with tears shed and emotions laid bare, I discovered a new kind of strength within myself—a strength born not only from combat experience but from the resilience and love of those who had my back, no matter the battle.

"My journey through cancer treatment was far from easy. Radiation presented challenges that required immense resilience. My doctor favored radiation therapy with chemotherapy at the same time to make radiation therapy work better.

"He ordered several weeks of external beam radiation therapy (EBRT) before surgery to make removing the cancer due to its size and location easier and to kill any rectal cancer cells that may be left behind.

"He explained that giving chemoradiation before surgery helped lower the chances of damaging the sphincter muscles in the rectum when surgery is done, and he wanted to treat nearby lymph nodes.

"My chemotherapy was given through a port, a central venous catheter, in cycles, followed by a rest period to give me time to recover from the effects of the drugs. These cycles were often 2 or 3 weeks long.

"Due to the type of drug I was given, the chemo was given for a few days in a row, and then, at the end of the cycle, the chemo was repeated to start the following process. The chemo was given for a total of 6 months.

"The physical toll of surgeries was relentless. After surgery, I needed a temporary ileostomy, which required a lifestyle adjustment and educating myself on how and where to order and manage the proper supplies.

"I responded well to the chemo but had several side effects. I lost my hair, had mouth sores, lost my appetite, and experienced nausea, vomiting, and diarrhea.

"Each treatment session brought a mix of emotions— hope, fear, and an unwavering desire to survive. My body fought a fierce war against the disease, and my spirit began wavering. Fear enveloped me like a blanket.

"I was physically and emotionally drained, so I sought comfort in my faith and the spiritual principles that had always been my guide. In difficult times, I had always relied on my strong beliefs, and now, as I faced the biggest challenge of my life, I needed that strength more than ever.

"I reached out to my Pastor, Reverend Joseph, who had always been a source of guidance for me. I confided in him about my fears, doubts, and the pain I was experiencing.

"Reverend Joseph listened with compassion and understanding, encouraging me to lean into my faith and use meditation and prayer to quiet my mind, connect with my inner self, and find comfort.

"At every step of the way, I found solace and strength in these disciplines and the support systems surrounding me. Family, friends, caregivers, and the virtual cancer support group at the C. W. Bill Young VA Medical Center in Bay Pines, FL.

"They rallied together, providing unwavering love, encouragement, and companionship. The power of these connections cannot be understated; they became my lifeline during the darkest moments, infusing me with hope and reminding me that I was not alone.

"As I continued my journey, my main goal was to make a lasting positive impact. I decided to use my struggles as motivation to help others who were going through similar challenges.

"My efforts included advocating for their needs, spreading awareness, and participating in cancer support groups as a guiding light of hope for future patients, inspiring them to fight with unwavering courage.

"As I navigated the ups and downs of my cancer journey, there were moments of reflection that brought clarity and perspective. I learned to appreciate the simple joys of life—the warmth of sunlight on my face, the laughter of loved ones, and the beauty of each passing day.

"These moments were reminders to cherish the present, find solace in the ordinary, and embrace the love and support surrounding me.

"My brave and determined effort was significant in the hearts of those I touched, a testament to my resilience, courage, and unwavering spirit. Although my physical body may have changed, my spirit inspires others to value life, treasure their loved ones, and persist in the fight against cancer."

Fear and anxiety are often constant companions when facing cancer. But with the right tools, strategies, and support, even those dragons can be slain.

FEAR/ANXIETY

The battle against cancer is a deeply personal and challenging journey that demands unwavering courage, resilience, and support. Through the story of Charlie's action, we are reminded of the strength of the human spirit, the power of love and support, and the profound impact one can have on the lives of others.

Let us honor his memory by continuing the fight against cancer, standing with those in their darkest moments, and holding onto hope in the face of adversity.

Receiving a cancer diagnosis can be a frightening experience that may cause fear, anxiety, and nervousness. Cancer affects physical health and emotions, which can be intense and unfamiliar.

These feelings may fluctuate throughout the day, including concerns about physical changes, caring for loved ones, finances, job security, and mortality. These emotions are normal for anyone undergoing treatment who has completed it or has a friend or family member experiencing it.

Veterans who are newly diagnosed with cancer and those who have been survivors for a long time have daily concerns. One of the concerns is the difficulty of planning for the future.

For example, it can be challenging to plan a family vacation when you are unsure of when you will undergo treatment. You may not feel well enough to commit to a lunch date, and some people hesitate to make plans.

It's understandable to feel concerned or anxious about the potential side effects of cancer treatment, such as pain, nausea, or fatigue. You may also be worried about relying on others for support or missing out on activities you enjoy. However, remaining flexible and acknowledging that plans may change is beneficial, as this approach works well for many veteran cancer patients.

I have seen long-term cancer survivors concerned about experiencing side effects from their cancer treatment months or even years after treatment. It's understandable for some to worry that the medicine may not be effective since it varies from person to person, even for those with the same type of cancer.

Additionally, those with cancer that has spread or those who have been using medication to control their cancer for an extended period may worry that their treatment will stop working.

It can be daunting to consider that specific treatments may work better for some individuals, and some may even have unwanted side effects. Also, the thought of a drug losing its effectiveness can be unsettling despite the availability of alternative treatment options. Comprehending your current and future treatment options is vital to prepare for what will come.

It is common to feel like life is out of control when diagnosed with cancer. This can be caused by various factors such as uncertainty about survival, disruptions to daily routines due to appointments and treatments, confusion from medical terminology, limitations on activities once enjoyed, and feelings of helplessness and isolation.

Dealing with the thought of death can be challenging. Feeling scared when contemplating mortality or losing a loved one is natural. It's common to experience death anxiety. It is essential to seek support during this challenging time and understand that experiencing these emotions is normal.

Fears and concerns about cancer are not uncommon, sometimes based on rumors, stories, or incorrect information. However, when cancer returns, cancer recurrence is a possibility even after successful treatment, which is a common fear among cancer survivors. If you're worried about it, you may want to take proactive measures.

Educating oneself about the facts can alleviate these fears. Understanding the specifics of the type of cancer diagnosis can help individuals become active participants in their care and feel less afraid.

Dealing with cancer can be influenced by one's upbringing and personal values. Some people may need to be strong and protect their loved ones, while others may seek support from family, friends, or other cancer survivors. Some may even turn to professionals or counselors, while others may find comfort in their faith.

It is important to remember that what works for one person may not work for another, so making decisions based on personal needs and not comparing oneself to others is essential. Loved ones may also experience similar emotions, and it can be helpful to confide in them if comfortable.

After beating a cancer diagnosis, individuals may experience a sense of hope. Many cancer survivors are living proof that holding onto hope is not just a possibility but a reality. The chances of living with cancer and overcoming it have never been better. Individuals with cancer can still maintain an active lifestyle even during treatment.

Research shows that individuals who are well-informed about their illness and treatment are more likely to adhere to their treatment plans and recover faster than those who are not. Doctors believe that hope may help the body deal with cancer.

The force of hope can be compelling, giving us the strength to persevere even through the most formidable obstacles. Numerous individuals throughout history have demonstrated how hope can guide us forward and empower us to conquer even the most daunting challenges.

The story of Charlie's triumph is an excellent reminder that hope can be a beneficial ally during life's most challenging trials. With hope in our hearts and a supportive community, we can endure and emerge stronger than ever.

CHAPTER FIVE

OVERCOMING THE DARKNESS

"Life isn't about waiting for the storm to pass...

It's about learning to dance in the rain."

—Vivian Greene

The emotional toll of being diagnosed with cancer can be overwhelming for anyone. Still, the burden may become even more complex for a veteran who has already endured the rigors of military service. Facing mortality while grappling with the trauma of war, a veteran diagnosed with cancer may find themselves succumbing to a mental health crisis.

However, this story focuses on the inspiring story of retired Air Force Master Sergeant Maxwell D, who circumvented the claws of depression and ultimately triumphed over adversity, proving that hope and resilience can prevail even in the darkest moments.

"My journey started last year in March '22. I saw two battle buddies retire as MSC officers from the 167 AES in Charleston, WV. I knew something was not quite right with my overall health.

"I had a colonoscopy the previous June before my mother's passing. Polyps and diverticula were noted and removed. No cancer was noted then.

"After returning from WV and MD, I had a lamb rib dinner at a restaurant. I started to have difficulty eating and swallowing the meal. I had scheduled a primary care visit in April, so I mentioned the situation to her.

"Diagnostics were scheduled, like the barium swallow and CT with contrast, later in April. Upper GI was planned for May, which noted esophageal cancer. Upon receiving the cancer diagnosis, my muscles tensed, I went numb, and I was paralyzed by fear and shock, unable to move or speak. My thoughts were bouncing around with "what ifs."

"The memories of past battles and the camaraderie shared with fellow airmen were juxtaposed against the uncertainty of the future. This collision of emotions (sadness, grief, anxiety, and fear) compounded my vulnerability, leading to a downward spiral toward depression. The constant thoughts of mortality and feelings of powerlessness threatened to engulf me.

"The month of June brought Community Care to consult at Moffitt Cancer Center for staging and port placement. My oncologist notified me that it was stage 4 with lymph nodes in the neck and axillary involved, spots on the left lung, and a spot on each lobe of the liver.

"Burdened by negative emotions, a sense of impending doom settled upon me like a heavy shroud, and I began withdrawing from those around me.

"I felt disconnected from friends and loved ones, unable to express the turmoil I was experiencing. Memories of war and the fear of the unknown in this battle with cancer made me believe that no one could truly understand what I was going through.

"July brought my course of treatment to the fore: FOLFOX and Keytruda. I wanted the best way to beat this. Genetic markers made Keytruda available. I had the first dosages at the end of July. My care teams at Bay Pines and Moffitt seemed to work well together. All the bills were being paid, and that worry was abated.

"August brought new challenges. My daughter's fiancé ended his struggle with depression by suicide at the end of July. After the funeral, she came for a week to stay with me. My third dosage was on the 15th, so she accompanied me.

"Good thing for me she did. We went to visit my other daughter in Largo for dinner. I felt like something was off on the way out to my car. Nausea was starting, as well as chills.

"I told my daughter to take me to Bay Pines VAMC Emergency room. My bad reaction to FOLFOX was just starting. I developed shivering so badly that I could not sign my name for admission. It felt like walking into a -60 degree freezer without clothes on. I developed infiltrates in the lungs and acidosis, turning me toxic.

"I went to the ICU and spent the rest of the week. The pump was discontinued on Tuesday earlier than the runtime was supposed to be since I convinced Dr. Shaikh that the reaction might abate without its presence.

"I met with Moffitt Cancer Center the following Tuesday to decide the next step in treatment. She felt it might be better to reduce the strength of the medication and give it over a longer time frame to see how that would be. So that is what we tried.

"The following Monday, 29 August, we tried again. The immunotherapy was done, and then the first of the chemo started and finished. Ten minutes into the flush, the reactions restarted with shaking and cold sensitivity. The shaking was worse this time.

"Petrified, I felt my trembling escalate into uncontrollable shivers. Barbiturates controlled the shaking until the bag was started. Ten minutes into the final part, the shivering returned. I turned febrile and nauseous and vomited.

"SICU became my new home for the next few days. I turned toxic again with acidosis and lung infiltrates again. It was worse this time since I also developed a pulmonary embolus in the lower right lobe of my lung.

"My bloodwork showed that all my blood values were tanking; lymph went from normal to 0.03, and white blood cells bottomed out, as did the red blood cells. I had difficulty breathing, and my oxygen saturation was low. A high-flow nasal cannula at 25 liters was done.

"I came out of the ICU to a step-down room on Thursday. I was discharged on Friday. I met Dr. Mehta the next week to discuss the next steps. We decided that chemo was not an option any longer. Recognizing that immunotherapy was the only option, my mental health teetered on the brink of full-blown depression.

"Admitting the severity of my emotional state, I took a courageous step forward and sought professional help. I contacted mental health counselors experienced in dealing with veterans' unique challenges.

"I started therapy and found a safe space to share my thoughts, fears, and vulnerabilities without judgment. This support proved a crucial turning point in my battle against cancer.

"With the guidance of mental health professionals, I learned various coping strategies to manage my symptoms. I found solace in creative outlets, such as painting and writing, which provided a healthy way to express my feelings and channel my energy. I practiced mindfulness and meditation to control my thoughts and emotions better.

"Additionally, I incorporated regular exercise of walking, yoga, swimming, and visiting the gym into my daily routine, which helped release endorphins and become a natural antidepressant.

"Being diagnosed with cancer posed a significant emotional challenge, but I faced it head-on and sought the support I needed. I gradually overcame my mental health challenges by seeking professional help, reconnecting with my veteran community, adopting coping strategies, and engaging in physical activities.

"I continue the Keytruda and Immune therapy. My marker numbers and scans have shown a smaller tumor in the esophagus and general improvement. There are one percent of cancer cells now in my blood. My care teams and the cancer support group have benefited my healing and growth. But it was my attention to my mental health that helped to get me over the finish line."

MENTAL HEALTH

Max's story reminds us that mental health challenges are not signs of weakness but a call for help and support. They can be overcome with proper assistance and a determined spirit, even when facing challenges like cancer. Max's triumph is a testament to the power of resilience and the importance of seeking help when facing the darkest times.

Many people with cancer may feel a lack of certainty about what the future holds. After a cancer diagnosis, you may feel your life is less secure than it once was. It is essential to ask for support when you are feeling this way. Dealing with the uncertainty of cancer can trigger various emotions, such as anxiety, anger, sadness, or fear.

These feelings may even manifest physically, causing sleeping difficulties or hindering focus at work. Coping with uncertainty is crucial in maintaining good health. To manage these emotions, it's essential to acknowledge that there are situations you can control and others you cannot.

While it may be challenging, letting go of things beyond your control and focusing on your reactions to events can be helpful. If uncertainty affects your daily life, do not hesitate to seek support.

Experiencing this range of emotions is common when dealing with cancer, whether it's your diagnosis or that of a loved one. If these emotions start affecting your daily life or persist for a long time, talking to a mental health counselor may be helpful. Counseling can be especially beneficial during times of uncertainty or change, such as starting or finishing cancer treatment.

Some veterans living with cancer may ponder spiritual questions that are not quickly answered. Questions like, "Why did I get cancer?" "What is the meaning of my life?" or "What happens after death?" Spiritual care, also known as spiritual support, can help you deal with your suffering, understand your cancer and its treatment, and prepare for an uncertain future.

Spiritual support can help you cope with symptoms and side effects that impact your mind, emotions, spirit, and physical body. You can receive spiritual support at any point in your treatment, regardless of your type or stage of cancer. This includes immediately after your diagnosis, during treatment, and after treatment.

A chaplain or spiritual care advisor can provide you with that much-needed spiritual care and support. They are a member of your healthcare team, and they can assist you in identifying sources of strength to help you cope. They can also help you prioritize what matters most during your cancer journey. Additionally, they are skilled in discussing life, death, legacy planning, and finding purpose.

Even if your emotions don't seem severe, seeking counseling can still be beneficial. Coping with cancer can be challenging for patients and caregivers, and just a few counseling sessions can significantly affect your well-being.

Starting a relationship with a counselor can be nerve-wracking. It can feel strange to discuss personal issues with someone new, even if they are a professional counselor. To ease any concerns, I recommend that you research and contact various mental health counselors before your first session. This will help you get a sense of how you would work together.

The effectiveness of counseling largely depends on the rapport you build with your counselor. Not all counselors or types of counseling may be the right fit for you. If you feel uncomfortable or don't see any progress after a few sessions, it is essential to discuss your concerns with your therapist and explore the possibility of finding a new provider.

If you decide not to speak with a therapist, consider contacting a local support group. Being part of a group can allow you to connect with others experiencing similar challenges to cancer. Additionally, confiding in close friends and family members you feel comfortable with can be beneficial.

Let them know how you feel and what kind of assistance you need. It's also important to educate yourself on cancer and its treatment options. Obtaining proper information and support can help you prepare for what lies ahead.

The stigma surrounding mental health can make it difficult to accept a diagnosis, but refusing treatment can lead to serious consequences such as delayed treatment and isolation. Therefore, intervention and support are crucial.

CHAPTER SIX

PATHWAY THROUGH THE SHADOWS

"God didn't promise days without pain, laughter without

sorrow, or sun without rain, but He did promise strength for

the day, comfort for the tears, and light for the way."

—Unknown

Cancer, a relentless adversary, has the power to disrupt lives, sow seeds of despair, and impose unimaginable suffering. This story explores the profound journey of a veteran patient bravely facing cancer, highlighting the emotional and physical toll of the disease while emphasizing the importance of compassion and support in such trying times.

"My name is Martha C, a 65-year-old Army veteran who, on July 27th, 2022, was told the results of an ultrasound would take about three weeks to come back. In my mind, I was saying, 'I am free of cancer.' However, I received a call the next day, and it was confirmed that I had a tumor on my right breast, and it was cancerous.

"When I received my cancer diagnosis, a horrifying wave of shock, fear, and a sense of helplessness crashed over me, sending tremors coursing through my body, rendering my legs weak and unstable.

"I sat there frozen in fear and uncertainty, wrestling with denial, anger, and sadness. The weight of doubt descended, and the arduous journey and battle began.

"I went through cancer denial because I thought, at 65, I had beat it since my family members were diagnosed between the ages of twenty-five and fifty. I was angry and in denial due to having a test done several years ago with a finding of a five percent likelihood of ever getting cancer; and now I had it.

"The mammogram was repeated, followed by Ultrasound, CT scan, PET Scan, labs, surgery, and biopsy — just a few tests I underwent. Words I had never heard of or understood came to me; for example, HER2 negative or positive, estrogen and progesterone receptors, hormone receptors, lymph nodes, markers, high and low beam Radiation, and so many more.

"I was told I had rare cancer that only about 7-11 percent of the population got. My diagnosis was a Malignant Neoplasm of the Right Breast, with the rare name Mucinous Carcinoma.

"I imagined various treatment options, each with its challenges. Chemotherapy, radiation, surgery, and immunotherapy came to my mind as the tools used in my fight against cancer.

"These treatments aim to weaken or eradicate cancer cells, but my oncologist told me Chemo would not help my cancer. So, on August 30th, 2022, with much anger inside me but no longer in denial, I had surgery.

"In that moment of terrifying clarity, I finally understood and accepted what God had allowed and didn't ask, "Why me, but why not me." I asked God not to let me go through Chemo, and he answered my prayer. I JUMPED FOR JOY!

"The surgery and medication heavily affected my physical and emotional well-being. I had surgery to remove the tumor and other affected areas on the scans, followed by radiation therapy directed at the specific area of the cancer and hormonal treatment to block or lower the amount of estrogen found in mucinous carcinoma of the breast.

"Side effects such as nausea, hair loss, fatigue, and pain tested my resilience, pushing me to my limits. The cancer's toll extended beyond the physical realm.

"I experienced an emotional roller coaster, battling anxiety, depression, and existential questions. The fear of the unknown, the loss of control, and the uncertainty surrounding the future weighed heavily on my mind. Sometimes, hope flickered like a candle in the wind, and I prayed for strength to keep moving forward.

"Amidst the pain and anguish, I found moments of solace and gratitude. My Pastor suggested I meditate and keep a journal. He encouraged me to write about my feelings, thoughts, and spiritual insights for clarity and depth.

"At first, I found it challenging to silence the worries and anxieties that plagued my thoughts. Still, with persistence and my Pastor's guidance, I gradually began to experience moments of tranquility and peace during meditation.

"Journaling brought me comfort and serenity as time passed. It allowed me to release my emotions, fears, and hopes. It helped me see progress in my spiritual journey during my struggles with cancer.

"I began to view my illness as an opportunity for growth and transformation rather than a burden to bear. My faith gave me the strength to face each day with renewed hope and determination.

"I also started attending spiritual gatherings at church and found a supportive community that embraced me openly. Sharing my journey with others on their healing paths brought a sense of connection and understanding I hadn't experienced before. I realized I was not alone in my struggles and that a web of support was woven around me.

"I began to see the beauty in each moment through my spiritual disciplines, cherishing the time I had left and using it to deepen my relationships with loved ones. I forgave those I once held grudges against and sought forgiveness from others, feeling the weight of old resentments lift from my heart.

"As the seasons changed, so did my perspective on life and cancer. The disease remains a part of me but no longer defines me.

"Cherishing my loved ones, relishing simple pleasures, and embracing the beauty of each passing day became my coping mechanisms. I yearned to leave a legacy, to be remembered for my courage, resilience, and the lessons I learned along the way.

"My support system played a crucial role throughout this tumultuous journey, ensuring my comfort and dignity, focusing on pain management and emotional support. Loved ones, friends, and healthcare professionals provided me with a safe harbor where I could express my fears, frustrations, and hopes.

"The unwavering support and understanding from my husband and loved ones provided solace during the darkest moments. I also received support from the cancer support group that meets weekly at the VA Medical Center at Bay Pines, FL.

"I met with other veteran cancer survivors and came to terms with my situation. They helped turn me back onto the positive side of the street—to rely on my faith and relationship with God to see me through.

"Though I am still in much pain and a lump has come back in the same breast, I know God's word, 'I will never leave nor forsake you,' will see me through anything thrown my way.

"My journey did not start and it won't end here. I still have a lot in life that I must accomplish."

For Martha, a veteran who served her country with unwavering courage and dedication, the battle with cancer was just the beginning. She developed the debilitating effects of cancer-induced lipidemia due to her cancer treatment.

The diagnosis was a shock, hitting deep in the pit of her stomach and knocking the wind from her sail as she was already dealing with the emotional upheaval of her cancer journey.

Lipidemia, also known as lymphedema, is characterized by tissue swelling due to the accumulation of lymphatic fluid. When cancerous tumors grow or spread to the lymph nodes, they can obstruct or damage the lymphatic system, resulting in lipidemia. This condition most commonly affects the arms and legs and can cause discomfort, pain, and limited mobility.

"Living with cancer-induced lipidemia presented me with new challenges. The swelling in my arms and legs made everyday activities like walking, standing, or even sitting for extended periods difficult and painful.

"Seeing how these activities are the best treatment for Lipidemia, I tried swimming, exercising in a pool, and riding a stationary bike to reduce the stress on my joints. I also started eating an anti-inflammatory, heart-healthy diet to slow its progression.

"The one thing I found that works best for me is wearing compression stockings that help increase‑ blood circulation in my arms and legs.

"As a result, I had to adapt to a new way of life that required immense courage, resilience, and support.

"This new chronic condition affected my mental health. I found myself grappling with feelings of frustration, sadness, and isolation. I longed for the physical freedom I once enjoyed and struggled to accept my new reality.

"However, I refused to let despair consume me, and I turned to my religious faith to provide a perspective that gave me comfort and fortitude.

"I found comfort and healing through my faith during my illness. I turned to it for answers to my questions, solace from fear and pain, and to find a purpose in challenges. My religious teachings taught me guidance about healing, not just curing, which helped me cope and find peace.

"I understood that medical treatments are not always effective and that spiritual and emotional healing can offer profound solace, especially when medical treatments fail.

"While my primary focus was to cure my cancer, I also realized the importance of healing my soul. I strived to align my values with my faith's teachings and recognized my life's values. I prayed for a successful recovery but also understood the significance of spiritual healing.

"I also sought professional help and again called on my tremendous and dedicated support system to cope with the emotional burden. My husband, fellow veterans, family, and friends rallied around me, offering emotional and practical support.

"They once again became pillars of strength during my darkest moments, proving that the power of community can make all the difference in one's battle against adversity.

"My determination to live a fulfilling life led me to explore various coping strategies and rehabilitation techniques. Physical therapy was crucial in managing my lipidemia symptoms, improving my mobility, and reducing pain. I regained some semblance of the life I once knew with time and effort.

"Despite facing numerous challenges, my spirit remained unyielding. I educated myself about cancer-induced lipidemia and the daily struggles that patients like me face. Through public records, support groups, and social media platforms, I learned the importance of early detection, support systems, and research in improving the lives of those living with lipidemia."

It's easy to allow devastating news to drag you down into the depths of denial. But facing negative health news is the best way to learn how to access the best health care, spiritual care, mental health care, and community support available.

DENIAL

Martha's journey as a veteran who battled cancer not once but twice is a poignant reminder of cancer's devastating impact on individuals and their loved ones. It illuminates the importance of empathy, compassion, and support in facing such adversity.

Through her determination, advocacy, and the unwavering support of her community, she inspires all those confronting life's most challenging battles. Her journey reminds us that while cancer and lipidemia may alter life's course, even claim lives, the will to live cannot be extinguished and remains stronger than any hardship.

As we reflect upon Martha's story, we can be inspired to advocate for early detection, advance medical research, and provide unwavering support to those fighting this relentless disease. The diagnosis can be shocking, and the fear of vulnerability can contribute to denial. The more we can do to provide options and hope, the better outcomes will be for those fighting these ailments.

The experience of a veteran diagnosed with cancer and remaining in a state of denial is a poignant and complex narrative that sheds light on the unique challenges faced by individuals who have dedicated their lives to serving their country.

Martha's emotional and psychological journey takes us into the depths of despair, highlighting the reasons behind her denial and its potential consequences on her health and well-being.

After going through the challenges of military service, veterans may perceive themselves as indestructible. However, a cancer diagnosis can shatter this perception and bring about a sense of shock that can be hard to handle.

Under these circumstances, denial can be viewed as a psychological defense mechanism that helps protect individuals from the harsh reality of the diagnosis.

Veterans may find it challenging to acknowledge their vulnerability when facing cancer, as they are accustomed to self-reliance and strength. Denial can become a coping mechanism to maintain control.

Denial can have serious consequences, particularly when it comes to seeking treatment. Veterans who refuse to accept their diagnosis may delay necessary medical interventions, allowing their cancer to progress to a more advanced and harder-to-treat stage.

Additionally, denial can cause emotional isolation as veterans may be reluctant to share their diagnosis or seek support from loved ones. This isolation can worsen loneliness and despair, further affecting their mental health.

Many veterans are reluctant to confess their emotional difficulties or seek assistance because they fear being seen as fragile or mentally unstable. This stereotype can make it even more difficult for veterans to recognize their cancer diagnosis and the emotional burden that comes with it.

It's common for veterans to carry unresolved trauma from their military service, and receiving a cancer diagnosis can cause traumatic memories to resurface or exacerbate ones they are already struggling to overcome. Some veterans use denial as a defense mechanism against these painful experiences.

To help veterans address their feelings and fears, it is important to create a safe and non-judgmental environment for them to express themselves. Communication with healthcare providers and loved ones can also help confront the diagnosis.

When a veteran is diagnosed with cancer but remains in denial, it can be a difficult and emotionally complicated journey. The diagnosis can be shocking, and the fear of vulnerability can contribute to denial.

The stigma surrounding mental health can make it difficult to accept a diagnosis, but refusing treatment can lead to serious consequences such as delayed treatment and isolation. Therefore, intervention and support are crucial.

A multidimensional approach is necessary to break the cycle of denial among veterans battling cancer. This approach must include open communication, access to mental health support, and a deep understanding of veterans' unique experiences.

By addressing these challenges, we can provide our veterans with the necessary help and support, honoring their service and sacrifice with the care and compassion they deserve.

CHAPTER SEVEN

MULTIPLE MYELOMA

"Cancer is a word, not a sentence."

—John Diamond

In the human spirit realm, few stories capture the essence of courage and resilience, like that of a long and courageous battle with multiple myeloma. Multiple myeloma is a formidable adversary, a rare and aggressive form of cancer that targets plasma cells within the bone marrow. Yet, in the face of this relentless foe, some individuals rise above the odds, defying expectations and inspiring others with unwavering determination.

Dick's journey begins with the life-altering moment of diagnosis. He was fulfilling, pursuing a successful career, and enjoying time with loved ones when fate dealt a heavy blow.

Life suddenly and unexpectedly took a turn as the cancer of multiple myeloma struck like a thunderclap, disrupting his life, shattering dreams, thrusting him into the uncharted territory of battling a complex and relentless disease and forever altering the course of his life.

"I was a Navy petty officer when I was diagnosed in my early thirties, which caused me to be medically discharged from active duty. Because of my age and health, I was told I could live with cancer for numerous years with treatment.

"Upon diagnosis, fear consumed me and wrapped its suffocating arms around me, rendering me speechless. Yet, amid these overwhelming emotions of anger, guilt, and uncertainty, I was determined to face the situation head-on.

"So, I confronted this overwhelming whirlwind of emotions by allowing myself to feel and express my anger healthily rather than holding it all in. I discussed my anger with a trusted family member who let me vent properly. I also did some physical exercises and wrote in my journal to help process my emotions.

"I was no stranger to challenges as a man known for my vivacity, optimism, and dedication. However, I could not have fathomed the magnitude of the test ahead.

"But, true to my character, I gathered my strength and embarked on a journey that would demand courage beyond measure. Multiple myeloma may be a formidable adversary, but it was no match for my determined spirit.

"My battle with multiple myeloma led me through a long, arduous treatment path marked by unpredictability and persistence. It was a labyrinth of chemotherapy sessions, stem cell transplantation, and numerous rounds of various medications.

"The road was laden with physical and emotional challenges, leading to moments of doubt and exhaustion. Each hurdle seemed more daunting than the last, but each obstacle became an opportunity for me to tap into newfound reservoirs of strength and resilience.

"Although my treatment regimen effectively treated multiple myeloma, it's not always curative. The success of the treatment depends on several factors, such as overall health, the cancer's stage and aggressiveness, and how the patient responds to the treatment.

"Regrettably, although my stem cell transplant was successful, the cancer returned. Yet, despite the hardships, I persisted, finding solace in the support of my loved ones and the compassion of my medical team.

"Cancer is a complex and challenging illness, and how people respond to treatment can differ. I continued collaborating with my medical professionals to explore other treatment options, assess their potential advantages, and set realistic expectations for my case.

"The oncology team evaluated various factors specific to my situation and developed the most suitable and effective treatment plan.

"I joined a clinical trial and underwent various treatments to combat cancer. I received specialized drugs, such as CD38 protein and B-cell maturation antigen (BCMA), which specifically targeted abnormalities in the cancer cells to prevent their growth and survival.

"Additionally, radiation therapy was administered to alleviate bone pain and address localized areas of the disease. Supportive measures were also implemented, including bisphosphonates to strengthen bones, erythropoietin to address anemia, and antibiotics to prevent infections and manage symptoms and complications.

"Four of us started this cancer journey together, but none of my fellow cancer friends were so fortunate. Their response to the treatment protocol didn't go the way they planned and they lost their battle against cancer.

"When diagnosed, people asked me how they could help. Accepting help at first was difficult because I felt good and didn't think I needed it. However, I soon realized that people offered help for me and themselves.

"They cared for and loved me, and helping me made them feel better. So, although I didn't require someone to drive me to my doctor's appointments, if a friend offered, I accepted. I understood the importance of receiving help for me and for those assisting me.

"Throughout my long battle, my support system proved a vital lifeline, bolstering the spirit and offering comfort. My family, friends, and caregivers became my pillars of strength, offering unwavering love, encouragement, and empathy.

"They rallied around me during the darkest hours of losing fellow veterans to cancer, lifting my spirits, addressing my guilt, and reminding me that I was not alone in this fight. Their genuine care and compassion became a source of inspiration, reinforcing the will to keep wrestling against the unseen enemy.

"My battle against multiple myeloma extended beyond medical treatments. I discovered the importance of nurturing the mind and spirit alongside the body. I embraced complementary therapies such as yoga, meditation, pastoral counseling, palliative care, and art therapy, finding moments of peace amid the chaos.

"These complementary therapies were not intended to cure cancer but to alleviate my discomfort, to provide a respite from the relentless cycle of treatments, and to nourish my mind and soul.

"In medical challenges, multiple myeloma is notorious for its unpredictability. I faced anxiety because I expected my scans to be routine. But then, once they started becoming abnormal, I developed anxiety about getting them.

"I wondered, what are the numbers going to be? Are my cancer markers back? Are they higher? Will there be holes in my bones that require escalated treatment?

"I fluctuated between hope and uncertainty, often accompanied by fear of the unknown. But I learned to cherish the good days, find joy in simple pleasures, and cherish moments with loved ones.

"I found purpose in empowering others on similar journeys as I pressed forward. I became an advocate, raising awareness about multiple myeloma and supporting initiatives to fund research for better treatments and, ultimately, a cure.

"My battle with multiple myeloma continues and is a testament to the power of the human spirit in the face of adversity. Throughout my journey, I try to display tenacity. Only fierce determination can transcend the boundaries of illness. So, I work to remain strong, inspiring those around me and reminding everyone I meet that courage knows no bounds.

"Though the battle is fraught with challenges, there is still a glimmer of hope in the darkest moments. And that very hope kindles the flames of courage, igniting a fierce determination to conquer even the most formidable foes. My story touches hearts far and wide, offering hope to those battling this formidable disease. I move forward with faith rather than succumbing to fear, doubt, or guilt."

GUILT

When a person is diagnosed with cancer survives the treatments, and learn to live with it, some feel grateful, while others experience a sense of guilt. You may question why you were spared or wonder why others diagnosed were not. This is known as "survivor guilt," an unofficial but natural phenomenon.

While not everyone experiences guilt, it is a feeling that is often challenging to overcome. Some people are more susceptible to it, such as those with a history of depression and low self-esteem.

Usually, survivor guilt is associated with catastrophic events, such as battlefield deaths or roadside bombs. However, it can also occur unexpectedly, like when someone receives a cancer diagnosis.

Dealing with the emotional effects of cancer can be a long-lasting struggle, even after active treatments have ended. You can't understand how to navigate all the emotions that come with being treated for cancer, becoming cancer-free, and losing family members while also trying to reconcile that you are grateful to be alive.

You are still here, and so many people diagnosed with cancer aren't, including people you met who had your type of cancer. Regardless of the type of cancer one is diagnosed with, it can lead to a complex mixture of feelings. Guilt is a common emotion experienced by many cancer survivors.

Many individuals who are battling cancer feel guilty. Guilt is a sensation of responsibility and remorse that can be difficult to acknowledge and voice out. It frequently urges people to repeatedly imagine "what if" and "if only" situations to identify what they might have done differently.

It is not uncommon for people with cancer to feel guilty for various reasons at different times. However, constantly fixating on these emotions can harm one's mental health.

Holding onto guilt for things you cannot control can ultimately lead to depression, which is common among cancer patients but should not be seen as a regular part of living with cancer. Repressing these feelings won't make them disappear. The goal isn't to eliminate guilt but to change your perspective. Letting go of feelings of guilt can improve your general well-being and make it easier to manage cancer.

Cancer patients may feel guilty about their past lifestyle choices, like smoking cigarettes. But it's important to let go of regrets or self-blame and offer forgiveness to oneself and others.

It's important to acknowledge that your guilt may fluctuate throughout your cancer diagnosis. However, there are ways to cope with these emotions. One option is to confide in a trusted individual, counselor, or social worker about guilt.

Joining a support group can also provide comfort in knowing others have experienced similar emotions. Additionally, focusing on positive aspects of your life and engaging in enjoyable activities can help alleviate guilt.

Consider expressing your emotions through creative outlets like music or art or writing down your thoughts and feelings. Remember, it's normal to feel guilty, but there are healthy ways to cope and move forward.

Survivor guilt can happen in many forms, not just with cancer. If you are experiencing survivor guilt, there are six things you can try to alleviate the feeling. Each requires patience and time, but these tips can help you cope with the guilt that may arise from your existence.

First, it is essential to ask yourself who is genuinely responsible. You should not take the blame if the loss were caused by forces out of your control. In combat, for example, a solider should not accept guilt when the blame lies elsewhere, such as the Syrian government or global forces like ISIS.

On the other hand, if the loss was caused by corporate leaders, ill-considered policies, or the market, you should not blame yourself if you are an employee affected by it. Mourning those who are lost is necessary, but you should not feel responsible for their loss.

At times, there is no one to blame. Natural disasters or random misfortunes can happen without any warning or prevention. However, we tend to feel responsible for these situations, overestimating how much we knew before they occurred.

We may think we should not have left our hair straightener plugged in or gotten into a car with faulty brakes. This distorted responsibility assessment is due to our inflated sense of personal responsibility.

When we feel guilty for events we couldn't have possibly known or prevented, guilt may function as a false sense of control. By taking on the burden of responsibility, we tell ourselves that the loss was not random or inconsequential. It is essential to understand that you cannot control every event in life, and it is okay to let go of the guilt and mourn the loss.

Feeling guilty may not feel great, but it can serve as protection. When we fall victim to unfair or chaotic circumstances, it can be easy to feel helpless and powerless. However, experiencing guilt allows us to take responsibility and control the situation.

Second, don't use guilt to avoid dealing with grief. Though it may seem more straightforward, avoiding your genuine emotions will only make things worse in the long run. It's okay to feel intense emotions, and there's no one right way to do it. Do what works for you, whether you want to scream, cry, journal, or be alone.

Third, remember that there are people who love and care about you. Even if you feel undeserving of survival, think about how devastated they would be if you were not here. Embrace the gift of survival and share it with those who love you. They deserve it.

Fourth, it's not a zero-sum game. Hidden beneath survivor guilt is the idea that there's only so much luck to go around and that benefiting from good fortune means that someone else is deprived of it. But luck is random.

The lottery is a perfect example of arbitrary luck: sometimes, no one has the winning lottery number; sometimes, multiple people share the prize. The chances of you specifically hitting it big aren't increased or decreased by anyone else's picks. It's hard to accept that there's no more excellent order to things, but once we do, we feel vindicated.

Fifth, consider doing something meaningful for someone else. Even if it's just a tiny act of kindness, it can motivate you toward purposeful action. Guilt is often associated with regrets about the past, but it can also drive positive change.

Feeling guilty motivates us to make things right and find ways to honor those who were lost. These actions help us alleviate some of our guilt and move toward a brighter future.

Lastly, it is important to prioritize self-care after experiencing a traumatic event or feeling left behind. This means taking care of your physical and emotional well-being by eating healthily, getting enough sleep, exercising, and seeking support from others. Although guilt can serve a purpose in motivating us to make amends, survivor guilt can be misplaced.

It is crucial to allow yourself to grieve your losses and remember that the situation was not your fault. Know that others are grateful that you are still here and that you can use your experience to help others in the future.

CHAPTER EIGHT

FIGHTING AGENT ORANGE

"Cancer didn't bring me to my knees, it brought me to

my feet."

—*Michael Douglas*

In the quiet corners of a cul-de-sac in Tampa, FL, an unassuming figure can be found waging a battle that transcends time and memories. A Vietnam War veteran, Tony P., carries the weight of an unseen battle within him long after the war ended.

Decades ago, Tony was a young and eager soldier, stepping onto the foreign shores of Vietnam believing he was fighting for his country and defending freedom. As a young soldier, he bravely fought on the front lines, enduring the horrors of war and witnessing the devastation caused by Agent Orange (Dioxin).

"Like many others, I was exposed to the deadly herbicide known as Agent Orange, which was sprayed across the dense jungles to defoliate the landscape and expose the Viet Cong guerrillas and the North Vietnamese Army, known as "Charlie," to U.S. forces.

"Little did I know that this encounter with the toxic chemical would set me in an emotional battle that would shape the rest of my life.

"I returned home, haunted by the memories of war, the comrades I had lost, and the traumatic experiences that forever altered my soul. However, it wasn't until much later, when I began experiencing a series of inexplicable health issues, that I realized the full impact of my exposure to Agent Orange.

"The symptoms started subtly—a persistent cough, unexplained fatigue, and occasional bouts of depression. Initially, I dismissed them as signs of aging or the inevitable consequences of war. But as time passed, my health deteriorated further, and I was in constant physical and emotional distress.

"Determined to find answers, I sought medical advice and discovered that my symptoms aligned with the long-term effects of exposure to Agent Orange. The reality hit me like a barrage of artillery fire—my body had become a battleground, where the lingering effects of war continued to wage their silent war against my health.

"I delved deeper into my research and learned about the numerous health conditions associated with Agent Orange exposure. The list was extensive—cancer, respiratory problems, diabetes, heart disease, and more. The magnitude of the damage inflicted by this chemical agent overwhelmed me, but it also fueled my determination to fight back.

"Hoping for support from the nation I had served, I applied for Agent Orange benefits. Yet, to my disbelief, my claim was repeatedly denied. I was caught in bureaucratic red tape and forgotten. With each rejection, a profound sense of betrayal and anger surged within me.

"I was not alone in my struggle as countless veterans like me fought their battles against Agent Orange's effects. Many had already succumbed to its toxic legacy, while others endured pain and suffering.

"Determined to have influence, I joined support groups for veterans affected by Agent Orange. There, I found comfort in connecting with others who shared similar experiences and understood the emotional toll it took.

"The stories they shared, the battles they fought together, became a lifeline for me, a source of strength and resilience as they navigated the uncertainties of their post-war lives.

"One group member, Tom, functions by taking a daily regimen of medications to control the plethora of health problems he says were caused by his exposure. 'The medications help, but you still hurt and suffer,' he said. He knew what he was talking about; his calendar is filled with doctors' appointments.

"However, the emotional battle was far from over. My health continued to decline, and I received a rating for peripheral neuropathy and colon cancer that was considered service-connected. The toll it took on my physical well-being became increasingly evident.

"The pain and frustration of my physical ailments and the memories of the war that haunted me threatened to consume my spirit. But I refused to surrender.

"With the support of my loved ones, I sought therapy and counseling to address the physical and emotional scars left by my time in Vietnam and the ongoing struggles with Agent Orange-related illnesses. Talking about my experiences and sharing my fears and vulnerabilities became a critical step toward healing.

"Through therapy, I discovered I had PTSD (post-traumatic stress disorder). I had suspected that I was suffering from the disorder because of the symptoms I was experiencing. The most prominent symptoms of PTSD were that I didn't sleep or slept too much.

"I got angry at things that made absolutely no sense to be angry at. Driving was a challenge because I drove a lot in Vietnam. When I came up to a bridge, I had a tough time.

"In therapy, I learned to change my thought process through cognitive behavior therapy and re-live traumatic incidents through exposure therapy. I also discovered the power of self-compassion and forgiveness.

"I realized that blaming myself for my exposure to Agent Orange served no purpose—it was a consequence of war, a battle fought on behalf of my country.

"Accepting this truth allowed me to shift my focus from self-blame to self-care, directing my energy toward advocating for fellow veterans and raising awareness about the lasting impact of Agent Orange.

"In my battle against Agent Orange, I found purpose. I channeled my pain into a force for change, determined to ensure that future generations of veterans would not endure the same suffering. I became a voice for those who could no longer speak, tirelessly advocating for better healthcare, research, and support for veterans affected by Agent Orange.

"I rallied fellow veterans, collaborated with organizations, shared my story in the media, and reached out to policymakers to bring attention to this issue that had silently ravaged the lives of so many. My fight was not just for myself but for the countless veterans who had returned home carrying the invisible scars of Agent Orange."

The physical and emotional battle with Agent Orange continues to be a part of Tony's life, but he refuses to let it define him. He fought in Vietnam with valor and bravery, and now he fights for his and his comrades' well-being.

He knew the final thing he needed to do was find closure to be at peace with himself. So, he and his support group decided to do something about it. They organized a trip to where it all began.

Tony P. and a group of veterans set sail on a fishing boat off the coast of Vietnam. Each carried an emotional burden from a war that had ended decades ago. They were on a mission to find closure. Tony, a former infantry soldier who patrolled the dense jungles of Vietnam, stood at the helm with determination and apprehension.

Beside him was Maria Rodriguez, a nurse who had tended to wounded soldiers in makeshift field hospitals. Despite wearing sunglasses, her eyes revealed excitement and trepidation as they cut through the calm waters, whipped by the salty breeze.

As the boat sailed farther from the shore, memories of the past began to resurface. The veterans exchanged knowing glances, their shared experiences forging an unbreakable bond. They were exposed to Agent Orange during the war, a toxic herbicide with long-lasting and devastating effects. Now, they were returning to where they had unwittingly faced this silent enemy.

Over the next few days, the group explored the coastline, visiting villages and connecting with the people whose lives had been forever altered by the war. They participated in healing ceremonies and listened to the stories of those who had survived the conflict.

The veterans found themselves confronting their past and becoming a source of support for the communities they encountered.

One evening, as the sun began to set in a fiery blaze of orange and pink, the group gathered around a crackling bonfire on the beach. With the waves as a backdrop and the stars overhead, they began to share their own stories. Each narrative was a thread in the tapestry of their collective experience, woven with pain, resilience, and a shared sense of duty.

Tony spoke of the harrowing jungle battles, where the air was thick with uncertainty and fear. Maria recounted the endless stream of wounded soldiers she had tended to, and her voice filled with sorrow and pride.

Other veterans shared their memories – the camaraderie that had sustained them, the scars that still haunted their dreams, and the struggles they had faced upon returning home.

As the stories flowed, tears mingled with the sand, and a sense of catharsis enveloped the group. The weight of their past began to lift, replaced by a renewed purpose. They realized that their journey was not just about confronting the ghosts of Agent Orange but also about forging connections, finding healing, and making a difference in the lives of others.

In the days that followed, the veterans collaborated with local organizations to initiate projects to improve the lives of those affected by the war's aftermath. They teamed with villagers to rebuild homes, plant crops, and create spaces for communal healing.

As they labored together, the barriers of language and culture seemed to dissolve, replaced by a shared commitment to building a better future.

When it was time to depart, the veterans left a lasting impact on the communities they had touched and a piece of their hearts. As the fishing boat sailed back towards the horizon, Tony and Maria stood again at the helm, their faces etched with a newfound sense of closure and purpose. The echoes of the past had transformed into a chorus of hope, resilience, and the enduring power of human connection.

Tony's support group proved to be an unstoppable force upon his return home. Their collective voice demanded justice and recognition, organizing protests, writing letters, and traveling to Washington, D.C., to plead their case to lawmakers and officials. Their unwavering spirit and resilience were a source of hope for others who had suffered in silence.

As media coverage increased and public support grew, the government could no longer ignore their pleas. Congressional hearings were held, and a national conversation began regarding the lasting impact of Agent Orange and the nation's responsibility toward its veterans.

After years of tireless efforts, the tide began to turn in their favor. The government acknowledged the connection between Agent Orange exposure and the veterans' health conditions, leading to new legislation that expanded benefits and healthcare coverage for those affected.

Tony's legacy is one of courage, resilience, and an unwavering pursuit of justice for those impacted by the insidious effects of Agent Orange.

AGENT ORANGE

Vietnam War saw the prolific use of Agent Orange, and decades after its use, the emotional responses still reverberate among veterans, their families, and the Vietnamese people, leaving behind a legacy of pain and suffering.

For Vietnam War veterans, the emotional journey has been complex and distressing, plagued with challenges. They were sent to war, believing they were serving their country, only to be exposed to an invisible enemy that would haunt them for the rest of their lives.

Many veterans suffer from physical ailments and chronic health issues, causing further emotional pain. The emotional scars often manifest as PTSD, depression, anxiety, and survivor's guilt.

The response to Agent Orange extends beyond the veterans themselves to their families. Spouses, children, and grandchildren have witnessed their loved ones suffer from various health issues, disabilities, and premature deaths, leaving them feeling helpless, afraid, and uncertain. The constant stress and financial strain caused by medical expenses impact their mental well-being.

The emotional toll on the Vietnamese people as a result of the use of Agent Orange is profound grief and injustice. The herbicide's use resulted in many birth defects, disabilities, long-term health issues, and environmental devastation, affecting generations of Vietnamese citizens.

The lack of accountability, responsibility, or adequate reparations from those responsible for the herbicide's use adds to their emotional anguish.

While the wounds inflicted by Agent Orange run deep, efforts are being made to address and heal the pain. Recognition and acknowledgment of the suffering caused by Agent Orange have gained traction, prompting governments and organizations to provide medical support and compensation to those affected.

Mental health services tailored to the unique needs of veterans, their families, and Vietnamese victims have become more accessible.

Addressing the emotional response to Agent Orange requires a multifaceted approach that includes acknowledgment, support, and compassion. Governments and chemical companies must take responsibility for their actions, providing those affected with medical care, financial assistance, and resources.

Mental health support should also be prioritized, offering counseling and therapy for veterans, their families, and Vietnamese victims.

Public awareness campaigns can help shed light on the stories of veterans and victims, humanizing their struggles and advocating for support and justice. Educating future generations about the consequences of environmental devastation and the emotional toll of war can foster a collective commitment to preventing such tragedies from recurring.

The response to Agent Orange is a poignant reminder of the profound impact of war and environmental disasters on individuals and communities. The suffering experienced by veterans, their families, and the Vietnamese people demands recognition, support, and healing.

Together, we can strive for a more compassionate and understanding future, honoring their resilience and valuing the emotional well-being of those affected by such tragedies.

CHAPTER NINE

LIVING WITH REGRETS

"Overcoming cancer awakens courage and confidence inside of
you that makes you want to live big, bold, and intentional
every day."

—Renee Ward

Cancer is a life-threatening disease that can often cause
veterans to reflect on their lives and feel various emotions,
particularly regret. Regrets can be a significant source of
distress for cancer patients, and receiving the right kind of
support can play an essential role in helping veterans
overcome regrets and find peace and acceptance.

139

Veterans often encounter difficulties and demonstrate bravery, selflessness, and heroism during service. However, their struggles may persist even after returning home. A cancer diagnosis, for instance, can trigger fresh obstacles and resurface long-buried emotions and remorse.

Gene O., a military veteran battling cancer, illustrates this scenario. He is grappling with past regrets while striving to recover and seek absolution.

"Throughout my life, I faced many challenges and obstacles. I served my country as a brave and devoted soldier, sacrificing and enduring hardships on the battlefield.

"Despite my determination to start anew upon returning home, I struggled with regrets and fears that weighed heavily on my soul. However, I remained steadfast and persevered through these difficulties.

"What I wasn't prepared for was a cancer diagnosis. Fear consumed me so heavily that my heart beat so hard in my chest that I saw the vibrating pulses through my thin shirt. It was like I left my body and watched the doctor make her announcement from high in the corner of the room.

"The heart-wrenching news sent shivers down my spine as I struggled with the harsh reality of my situation. I was diagnosed with Stage 4 Esophageal Cancer, and my treatment regimen would consist of chemotherapy with Carbo/Taxol, numerous radiation treatments, and an esophagectomy if needed. Following the surgery, I would begin immunotherapy with Nivolumab for four weeks and three more chemotherapy treatments.

"These treatments aimed to weaken or eradicate cancer cells but took a heavy toll on my physical and emotional well-being. The side effects of nausea, hair loss, fatigue, and pain tested my resilience, pushing me to my limits.

"Fear of the unknown future, thoughts about mortality, and concerns about treatment options and their efficacy added to my emotional turmoil.

"When diagnosed with cancer, I struggled to balance fighting the disease with facing past regrets. I experienced various emotions: sadness, anger, and guilt. The mixture of emotions made my healing journey even more complex and challenging.

"It was a significant moment for me to face my unresolved issues from the past and come to terms with my diagnosis. Despite trying to conceal my regrets and maintain a stern demeanor, I eventually realized the need to address them. So, I channeled my energy into my work, hoping to keep myself distracted.

"However, no matter how busy I was, my regrets followed me like ghosts, haunting me constantly so I couldn't shake the feeling of remorse inside.

"Anxiety and depression also became my unwelcome companions, fueled by the ongoing medical appointments and treatments, the constant uncertainty of the outcome, my changed identity, and the potential impact on my social relationships.

"As I navigated the complex emotional landscape of diagnosis, some of my past regrets slowed down my ability to acknowledge the medical challenges while actively seeking ways to adapt and overcome them.

"By focusing on regrets, various coping strategies were ignored on my journey through cancer treatment, making it more difficult to find meaning in the face of adversity. So, I started focusing on one day at a time, celebrating small victories, and nurturing a positive mindset to increase my resilience and propel myself forward.

"I sought information to understand the type of cancer, available treatment options, and prognosis to gain control and empower me to make informed decisions.

"Emotional support from friends, family, and support groups provided a much-needed safety net during this challenging time. Additionally, adopting mindfulness practices, engaging in hobbies, and maintaining a healthy lifestyle positively contributed to my emotional well-being.

"Having dealt with my cancer diagnosis, I once again started thinking about the regrets in my life. One of my greatest regrets was not being present for my family during deployment.

"While deployments are crucial, as they serve the noble purpose of protecting the nation's interests and ensuring global security, being parted from my loved ones, family occasions, and cherished moments such as missed birthdays, anniversaries, and other milestones caused me deep guilt. This led to an internal conflict between my duty to my country and my loved ones.

"Another of my significant regrets was connected to my experience on the battlefield. I had seen the atrocities of war, and those haunting memories lingered with me like an indelible nightmare. I felt sorry for some of the things that happened while I was in the military.

"My regrets were linked to actions or inactions, especially the memories of fallen comrades or tough decisions made under extreme conditions during combat. These regrets became a heavy burden, causing me to experience guilt and shame.

"The loss of comrades and the inability to protect them haunted my dreams, causing restless nights filled with anxiety. I pondered whether alternative actions could have been taken to safeguard my fellow soldiers.

145

"I harbored feelings of regret that extended beyond my family and military career, affecting every aspect of my life. I constantly worried about falling short and letting others down, believing I could never meet their expectations. Furthermore, I was worried about my health and the possible long-term consequences of my service in the war.

"My regrets and fears started taking a toll on my overall well-being as time passed. I faced difficulty sharing my struggles with others, as I was apprehensive about burdening them with my emotions. Consequently, I began to distance myself from the world and became more isolated, all while putting up a façade of strength.

"I don't know how, but I stumbled upon a support group for veterans led by a Chaplain one day. Initially, I was unsure what to expect, but I tried it anyway. Sitting among my fellow veterans, I realized I wasn't the only one dealing with regrets and fears. Their experiences moved me deeply, and I could see the pain and resilience etched on their faces.

"I received invaluable support from the chaplain in overcoming my regrets. The chaplain created a safe and non-judgmental environment for me to express my emotions freely. With active and empathetic listening, the chaplain skillfully guided me to examine my life and identify the regrets holding me back. This helped me process my emotions and eventually move toward acceptance.

"I discovered through the support group that facing regrets and fears takes courage, not weakness. By sharing my experiences, I broke down the walls I had erected around myself. Hearing the stories of others provided me with a sense of connection and understanding that I had been lacking.

"I kept going to therapy sessions with a compassionate and understanding chaplain who patiently helped me deal with my regrets and fears. During our sessions, I learned to forgive myself for my mistakes in the past and acknowledge my humanity. Although I couldn't alter what happened, I realized I could improve by making up for my mistakes and being there for my loved ones.

"After years of being haunted by past regrets, I realized that the first step towards healing was acknowledging them. Confronting my past and the actions that had left scars on my conscience took immense courage.

"However, by sharing my emotions with trusted friends, family, and a therapist, I found a safe space to express myself and begin the process of self-forgiveness.

"During my turbulent emotional period, I discovered the importance of self-compassion. I acknowledged my humanity and the challenges I faced while serving my country. Recognizing my imperfections and admitting that I did my best under the circumstances helped ease my feelings of guilt.

"I developed techniques to handle my anxiety and unwanted memories. I courageously faced my fears and sought professional aid for my nightmares. Furthermore, I began to practice mindfulness to stay centered in the present moment.

"As time passed, my anxiety and regrets gradually lessened. I understood that the path to recovery was an ongoing process, and I was no longer afraid to face it head-on. I appreciated the encouragement of my fellow veterans, family, and friends, knowing they were there for me just as I was there for them. While I understand that some actions cannot be undone, I focus on making amends in the present.

"I find redemption through acts of kindness, community service, and supporting fellow veterans. These actions allow me to give back to society and move forward with closure.

"My struggle with regrets and fears changed me, not into someone who had conquered my past but into someone who had learned to bear it with fortitude and perseverance. My experience proved the strength of confronting inner demons, seeking solace in others, and striving for healing and redemption despite adversity.

"Being told I had cancer was a watershed moment that profoundly reshaped my life's course. The emotional rollercoaster, coping strategies, psychological impact, and the emergence of resilience all played a pivotal role in my transformative journey.

"While the path ahead was arduous, I understood that a cancer diagnosis did not define me. And the path to healing did not include wallowing in regret. By seeking support, embracing resilience, and focusing on holistic well-being, I could navigate the uncharted waters of a cancer diagnosis with strength and determination. And I could find ways to good in the world."

REGRETS

Life can be unpredictable, with unexpected twists and turns; for veterans who have faced challenges on the battlefield, dealing with unforeseen battles on the home front can be even more complicated. A cancer diagnosis can leave veterans feeling devastated, struggling with regrets from the past and uncertainty about the future.

Gene's story depicts the emotional journey of a veteran who is diagnosed with cancer. It delves into how he handled his doubts, regrets, and memories of lost comrades and the haunting question of "what if" during this challenging period.

Veterans often feel guilt and self-blame due to past decisions and missed opportunities, which can be even more challenging when facing a life-threatening illness like cancer. This can make it tough to accept their diagnosis and come to terms with the reality of the situation.

Getting diagnosed with cancer can trigger many worries about the future. Will the individual be able to overcome this new obstacle? How will it impact their loved ones? Coping with the physical and emotional strain of treatment can be challenging. The unknown can feel overwhelming and add to stress and anxiety.

Acknowledging worries and seeking professional assistance is crucial for addressing regret and uncertainty. For veterans, finding comfort in speaking with therapists, counselors, or support groups that specialize in cancer-related issues or mental health is essential. Discussing their emotions and fears with someone who understands their unique experiences can be incredibly helpful.

When veterans receive a cancer diagnosis, they may struggle with past regrets and doubts about their future. It is important to remember that they are not alone on this journey.

To confront the emotional challenges of cancer, veterans can find strength by seeking professional help, practicing self-compassion, engaging in support networks, and focusing on the present. With the support of loved ones and fellow veterans, they can navigate this difficult chapter and emerge stronger and wiser.

The experience of a cancer patient, a veteran living with regret, involves deep self-reflection, healing, and redemption. It is challenging to confront past mistakes while fighting a life-threatening illness.

However, finding healing with perseverance and a strong support system is possible. Throughout the journey towards redemption, the individual must understand the necessity of self-forgiveness and seeking forgiveness from others, as it can bring about profound healing.

Facing cancer can be a difficult challenge, but it may also provide an opportunity to come to terms with past regrets. The journey to recovery is not always straightforward, and setbacks may occur.

However, with the help of loved ones, a strong spirit, and a willingness to confront regrets directly, our veteran cancer patients can emerge from the experience with greater clarity, inner peace, and purpose for their future.

CHAPTER TEN

LUNG CANCER

"Cancer does not define who I am, although it is a significant part of me and who I am becoming."

—*Carrie Kreiswirth*

In the face of life's most formidable challenges, the power of faith can often be the driving force that propels individuals to overcome adversity. William Conner., a Muslim veteran who, armed with the teachings of Islam, demonstrated this faith poignantly by embarking on a profound journey to combat lung cancer.

155

This narrative showcases how faith becomes an unwavering source of inspiration, resilience, and determination for Bill in his battle against a relentless foe.

Nestled among the rolling hills of South Carolina, William (Bill), now age 56, grew up in the small rural town of Johnson, surrounded by tobacco farms where smoking was the drug of choice among several family members.

He remembers when he first lit a cigarette at 12 and nearly choked to death – but became a regular smoker after turning 16.

"It was not only my family; my friends did it too, which helped influence me to get started.

"I grew up in a household with siblings where military service spread over several generations. My family dedicated much of their life to serving our country, so I possessed a unique blend of discipline, courage, and resilience courtesy of my role models.

"My military upbringing forged a character accustomed to confronting challenges head-on, a trait that proved invaluable as I navigated the complexities of a cancer diagnosis.

"After graduating high school, I went off to the army, serving as a supply sergeant in the military for eight years, stationed in Fort Lee, Virginia, and then overseas in Germany.

"It wasn't unusual to smoke in the military, as the stress of the job needed relief; I went through nearly a pack of cigarettes daily at the height of smoking.

"I smoked my entire time in the army and would have continued, but that changed when I joined the Islamic faith and decided to leave military service. My Islamic faith emerged as a powerful source of strength. Islam's teachings emphasize patience (sabr) and trust in God's plan (tawakkul), which provide solace and resilience.

"Life was good following my time in the army. I used the GI Bill to attend school and continued to grow in my newfound faith. I enjoyed being a college student, even if it meant money was tight. But life as I knew it changed forever on the Fourth of July weekend in 2018.

"I had been feeling sick for a while and thought I had a stomach virus and tried to treat it myself with over-the-counter medication.

"Eventually, I went to my primary care doctor at the C. W. Bill Young VA Medical Center, who wanted a scan to ensure I didn't have kidney stones. That's when he found something that didn't look right and referred me for more testing.

"Further testing revealed what no one could truly prepare for. I couldn't have imagined my most challenging battle wouldn't be in service to my country. It came when I was diagnosed with stage 2 non-small cell lung cancer that had spread to my lymph nodes.

"I confronted the haunting specter of uncertainty as the battleground shifted from the combat field to my body's inner recesses. The diagnosis struck like a shockwave and was a life-altering event, shattering the illusion of invincibility cultivated through years of military service.

"Endless hospital corridors became the new trenches where battles were waged against fatigue, pain, and despair. Yet, amidst the struggle, my spirit remained unbroken. The courage that once propelled me through chaos and danger fueled my determination to face this new adversary head-on.

"My wife, Fatima, stayed at my side the entire time. She had been my anchor through countless challenges, supporting me during my military service and the subsequent battles with post-traumatic stress. Now, facing a cancer diagnosis, we were on the precipice of a new trial neither of us had anticipated.

"With a heavy heart, I told my wife, Fatima, 'We're facing a difficult journey ahead, but we must remember that Allah's plan is always for the best.'

"William,' she said, 'You're right; our faith has always guided us and will also see us through this.'

"Drawing on my faith, I found the inner strength to navigate the uncertainties and trials accompanying a cancer diagnosis. I found solace in my prayers, reading the Quran, and seeking support from my community.

"During these moments of vulnerability, my true faith and strength shone through. I met each procedure and setback with resolve and pushed forward to conquer the odds as I had so many times before.

"For me, the diagnosis became a profound test of faith, an opportunity to embody the teachings of Islam that emphasize patience (sabr), gratitude (shukr), and reliance on God (tawakkul).

"Islam, a faith that integrates seamlessly into every facet of life, provides a guiding light for me. The concept of trials (fitnah) is deeply ingrained in Islamic teachings, reminding believers that adversity is a natural part of existence. Drawing from the stories of prophets and role models who endured their trials, I realized I was not alone in my struggle.

"Patience (sabr) is a cornerstone of Islamic teachings and became a central tenet of my battle against cancer. Enduring the challenges of treatments, side effects, and emotional turmoil, I invoked sabr as a shield against despair. My resilience, nurtured by faith, enables me to persevere and maintain a positive outlook.

"Cancer was nothing new to me despite never having been diagnosed before. I lost a brother to cancer stemming from Agent Orange, a cousin from prostate cancer, and a close friend from lung cancer. One of my fellow soldiers also had lung cancer but survived.

"So, I underwent surgery at the VA Medical Center, followed by months of chemotherapy, radiation, and targeted therapies at Moffitt Cancer Center. The days of treatment were long and arduous, a ceaseless march through a landscape of uncertainty.

"Chemotherapy, surgeries, and radiation left their marks, physical and emotional. I started with them removing my left lower lobe and surrounding lymph nodes to check for signs of cancer, followed by chemotherapy using the drug Erlotinib intravenously for five days for three weeks to kill cancerous cells. I was then started on immunotherapy drugs to help my immune system fight any remaining cancer cells.

"My willingness to collaborate with healthcare professionals demonstrated my commitment to regaining control over my health. Even after treatment, I still went in to have scans and blood work done every few weeks.

"I tried to heal and put my life back together. Since no warrior fights alone, my family and community rallied around me, providing unwavering support. In Islamic culture, the concept of Ummah – the global community of Muslims – is deeply rooted. It is a testament to the strength of collective support.

"My battle against lung cancer becomes a shared journey as friends, family, and fellow believers rally around me with prayers, encouragement, and assistance. The outpouring of love, prayers, and service from fellow believers exemplifies the strength of this interconnected community. This community solidarity reinforced my faith and determination.

"During my treatment at Moffitt, my oncologist told me about a clinical trial testing a drug that showed promising results for some lung cancer patients. However, I didn't qualify to participate due to a newly discovered heart condition.

"Despite the disappointment, I persevered and learned to live as a cancer survivor. I enjoyed quality time with my family and got as involved as possible with my Mosque. And then, a glimmer of hope pierced through the storm clouds.

"The Oncologist said 'remission' - a word laden with relief, yet also with the weight of all that had been endured. It was a sunrise after a seemingly endless night, a beacon of triumph that spoke of resilience and the tenacity of the human spirit. I emerged from the shadows of illness, battle-scared but stronger, a living embodiment of the will to survive.

"In remission, I found a new lease on life, a chance to savor the everyday moments that once might have been taken for granted. The taste of victory mingled with the sweetness of each sunrise, the laughter of loved ones, and the simple joys of being alive.

"Every step was a testament to my determination, a victory lap that celebrated not just the survival of the body but the preservation of the soul.

"As the months turned into years, I was hopeful the cancer would remain in remission. However, that all changed again in 2020. When my brother died from cancer, I returned to Moffitt and saw Dr. Norman in December 2020.

"I expressed how I was in so much pain that my primary care doctor thought it was scar tissue, but Dr. Norman did scans just to be safe.

"Those scans once again revealed what I feared – the cancer had returned and now was categorized as stage 4 terminal lung cancer. My family, not wanting to lose me, became very hysterical. I couldn't hold back either, and my emotions flowed like a rainstorm.

"I grew scared and thought about all the things I didn't want to think about. Despite my fear, I had faith, believed in

God, and knew who was in charge and that I was not walking this journey alone. I let my faith calm me, and my community embraced me.

"As I began my chemo and radiation treatment, I found solace in my prayers, reading the Quran, and seeking support from my community.

"I weakly told Fatima, 'Sometimes I feel overwhelmed by the pain and uncertainty.' Fatima held my hand and said, 'Bill, let's recite Surah Ash-Sharh (Chapter 94) together.' One phrase stood out: 'Verily, with hardship comes ease.'

"As my treatment continued, our faith grew stronger, and we inspired each other and those around us with our unwavering trust in Allah's plan.

"I began to see my diagnosis not as an insurmountable enemy but as another chapter in my journey. I realized that just as I had faced adversity on the battlefield, I could meet this new challenge again with the same determination and resilience.

"Following the diagnosis, the pharmacist told me that the drug previously offered in the trial, which I didn't qualify for in 2018, had been approved. I was prescribed this drug and took it for the next two years. I felt amazing as it helped reduce the pain I was having.

"In late 2022, nearly two years after beginning my new drug, my scans showed the cancer was circumventing treatment and growing. A chill swept over my body as I grew anxious, uncomfortable, and worried about the new situation. So, I endured months of radiation, chemotherapy, and targeted drug treatment and remained optimistic.

"Every day, I feel so grateful to have another day. Even on my worst days, when I have trouble getting out of bed, I feel thankful to be alive. Cancer made me look differently at life.

"I still receive maintenance chemotherapy at Moffitt. I don't know how much time I have left, but I am at peace with my diagnosis and treatment, knowing I can now help others through their cancer journeys.

"I want my story to bring cancer awareness to attention so more people can understand and cope with taking their family members' health concerns more seriously. It would save more lives if people were more aware and knew what to look for."

This is a story of courage. But it is more than that. It is about the ability to bounce back from difficulty again and again. That is the heart of resilience all those dealing with cancer can access to continue holding on to hope.

RESILIENCE

Bill's triumph over cancer was more than a victory over disease; it was a victory over fear, doubt, and despair. And as Bill and Fatima stand at the precipice of the future, they carry a legacy of strength that will inspire future generations, illuminating a path of hope for others facing similar challenges.

By openly embracing his faith and sharing his journey, he inspires fellow veterans to draw strength from their spirituality when confronting life's adversities.

When cancer patients receive their diagnosis, they often feel weighed down by society's judgment of them. Loved ones, employers, and others may start treating them differently, causing fear and anxiety to linger with each visit to the doctor's office. Understanding the emotional stages that cancer patients go through can help them cope with the awareness of mortality that cancer brings.

Some cancer patients find that the prospect of death inspires creativity and brings loved ones closer together. Unfortunately, society shuns the thought of dying and often turns away from those with chronic illnesses like cancer.

However, it's essential to recognize that medical technology has dramatically extended life expectancy; those with serious illnesses can still lead fulfilling lives. Acceptance and understanding of the threat to life can help individuals deal with the emotional challenges of such diseases. Ultimately, life will prevail over death.

Not everyone will experience the same emotional reactions when dealing with a chronic, potentially fatal disease like cancer. Some may feel more than others. While it's helpful to be aware of these emotions, understanding them can help us face our uncertainties and make informed decisions.

Acknowledging our emotional response to a long-term illness that may involve periods of remission and a chance for recovery will allow us to prioritize our emotional well-being as our healthcare team focuses on our physical health. Our loved ones can provide valuable support to help us navigate this challenging time.

With their help, we can regain confidence, find avenues to cope with fear and anxiety, discover new sources of meaning and fulfillment, experience satisfaction, and ultimately achieve peace of mind.

Once the initial shock of a cancer diagnosis wears off, the focus shifts to receiving the best possible treatment. Patients educate themselves about their cancer, including its stage, prognosis, necessary tests, and available treatments. They also inquire about alternative treatments and weigh the advantages, disadvantages, and risks.

Apart from medical knowledge, patients also assess their strengths, weaknesses, spiritual beliefs, and support system. By gathering all this information, patients can develop a positive mindset, adapt to their situation, and lead physically and emotionally productive lives.

CHAPTER ELEVEN

RADIATION EXPOSURE

"Our life doesn't end the minute we get that diagnosis.

We still have some living to do."

—*Shannon Doherty*

Cancer is a formidable opponent that affects people of all ages, genders, and backgrounds worldwide. Many brave military veterans who have already overcome challenges in their service to their country are also facing this disease.

This story tells the inspiring tale of Alex, a Navy veteran fighting leukemia. His battle is made even more difficult by his past exposure to radiation during his service. Alex's journey highlights the resilience, strength, and determination of those who have served their country and now face a new challenge.

"My story starts with my dedication to serving my country. As an armed forces member, I was exposed to numerous hazards, including radiation. Whether operating machinery, working in close quarters with electronic equipment, or being stationed in areas with potential radiation exposure, my service brought me into contact with various radiation sources.

"I spent years serving my country in the Nav. However, despite leaving the military, I faced a new and unexpected battle vastly different from my experiences at sea. I received a leukemia diagnosis that would change my life.

"Medical examinations revealed that my illness directly resulted from my past radiation exposure. The diagnosis was a blow when I was first diagnosed. Shock, anger, fear, guilt, and denial were all expressed, but an incredible display of courage and determination followed.

"The emotional impact of a blood cancer diagnosis can often be just as complex, if not more challenging to cope with, than the physical aspects of the disease. However, my military training and experiences equipped me with a unique mental fortitude, enabling me to face these challenges head-on.

"So, I educated myself about my disease and the best weapons to use against it. I learned that leukemia is a type of cancer that affects the tissues responsible for forming blood, including the bone marrow and lymphatic system.

"I discovered that blood has three types of cells: white blood cells that fight infection, red blood cells that carry oxygen, and platelets that help blood clot.

"My bone marrow makes billions of new blood cells daily, primarily red. When I was diagnosed with leukemia, my body

175

produced more white cells than it needed. These leukemia cells can't fight infection like normal white blood cells.

"Because there are so many of them, they affect how my organs work. Over time, I didn't have enough red blood cells to supply oxygen, enough platelets to clot my blood, or enough normal white blood cells to fight infection.

"Treating leukemia can be complicated and depends on many factors, such as the type of leukemia you have, how far it has spread, and your overall health will determine the treatment options available.

"The main treatment options include chemotherapy, radiation, biologic therapy, targeted therapy, stem cell transplant, and surgery. These various strategies and resources can help make the treatment successful.

"Treatment for leukemia commonly involves chemotherapy, which involves using drugs to eliminate cancer cells in the blood and bone marrow. This medication can be administered either through a shot into a vein or muscle, as a pill, or directly into the fluid around the spinal cord.

"Radiation therapy, on the other hand, uses high-energy X-rays to destroy leukemia cells or prevent their growth. This treatment can be applied to the entire body or a specific area where cancer cells are concentrated.

"Immunotherapy, also known as biologic therapy, is a treatment that assists your immune system in identifying and attacking cancer cells. Interleukins and interferon are two drugs that can enhance your body's natural defense mechanisms against leukemia.

"Targeted therapy utilizes drugs that block specific genes or proteins that cancer cells require to grow. This treatment can halt leukemia cells' signals to grow and divide, cut off their blood supply, or kill them directly.

"A stem cell transplant is a procedure that replaces leukemia cells in your bone marrow with new ones that can produce blood. Your doctor can extract the new stem cells from your body or a donor.

"Initially, I received high doses of chemotherapy to eliminate the cancer cells in my bone marrow. The new stem cells were infused into one of my veins, growing into new, healthy blood cells.

"If needed, I would have opted for surgery. If my spleen filled with cancer cells and put pressure on neighboring organs, my doctor would perform a splenectomy to remove it. I chose to undergo Immunotherapy to battle against this invading enemy.

"Battling leukemia was a challenging experience for me, both physically and emotionally. I experienced various emotions throughout my prolonged treatment, and the disease significantly impacted my overall well-being.

"Mentally, I struggled to cope with the side effects of treatment, the uncertainty of my prognosis, and the psychological impact of the diagnosis, pushing my resilience to the limit.

"I experienced cancer fatigue as a significant symptom while battling leukemia. It was distinct from regular tiredness, despite my efforts to rest and limit my activity. To manage this fatigue during my treatment, I reached out for help and welcomed the support of others.

"My doctor recommended alternative therapies such as meditation, yoga, and deep breathing exercises to alleviate his fatigue.

"I was a military person who also suffered from significant pain caused by leukemia. Though I tried to bear it bravely, the pain became unbearable. I approached my oncologist, seeking help to manage it.

"The oncologist understood that pain can severely impact both emotional and physical health. He conducted a question-and-answer session to determine the type and level of pain that I was experiencing. He ruled out bone pain caused by overactive bone marrow and identified neuropathic pain as nerve pain.

"The oncologist prescribed non-opioid pain medications, acupuncture, massage, transcutaneous electrical nerve stimulation (TENS), and interventional pain techniques like nerve blocks and spinal cord stimulation.

"Stress management techniques were also recommended. The oncologist said he would refer me to a pain management specialist if the pain became unbearable.

"When battling cancer, having a solid support network is crucial. I found this out the hard way. A few of my close friends came around less and less because they were unsure how to deal with the situation. My family also treated me differently because of the cancer and the new normal.

"But they reminded me they would be there and do whatever it took to help me get through this medical situation.

It took much communication, but my family and I could set and reinforce boundaries regarding my treatment regimen.

"I sincerely and calmly thanked my family for their suggestions but let them know that, ultimately, it was my decision regarding my treatment.

"I discovered that the most effective emotional support came from others who had experienced leukemia or cancer firsthand. So, I joined a cancer support group at the C.W. Bill Young VA Medical Center and found it incredibly valuable. There, I was able to connect with others who were facing the same challenges as me.

"I also had the support of friends, family, fellow veterans, and medical professionals who rallied behind me. Their unwavering support became essential to my journey, offering encouragement and empathy during despair.

"During my leukemia treatment, my doctors advised special precautions for family and friends visiting as it could put me at risk of infection. To stay in touch during my isolation, phone calls, video calls, texts, and emails were recommended, significantly impacting my emotional well-being.

"I used my cancer journey as a platform to advocate and raise awareness about the potential health risks military personnel face from radiation exposure during their service.

"I shared my story to shed light on the issue and aimed to improve safety protocols, increase awareness, and ensure that the sacrifices made by servicemen and women do not lead to unnecessary health battles."

Alex's experience showcases people's strength in the most difficult situations, particularly those who have served their country.

Additionally, it highlights the significance of continuous research, education, and assistance for veterans who encounter health issues due to exposure during their service.

As we salute Alex's bravery and determination, let his story remind us that the human spirit remains indomitable despite daunting odds. Through advocating for better practices and raising awareness, his journey contributes to a future where veterans like him can lead healthier lives after their dedicated service to their nation.

He made the wise choice of including his family and support system. Still, he endured the bitter reality that people who are scared or uncomfortable often stay away when a friend is diagnosed and their health begins to decline.

ISOLATION

Dealing with leukemia can be physically and emotionally challenging and impact mental health. After undergoing cancer treatment, many survivors notice that the world tends to fall short in supporting some individuals. During treatment, every aspect of life is highly structured and recorded. Medications are meticulously scheduled, and medical professionals regularly monitor their progress.

Frequent lab tests are conducted to keep track of their health. They're also given a list of phone numbers to contact in case of any side effects. Despite all this, support from loved ones and healthcare providers is essential.

As time passes, the inquiry about their well-being starts to dwindle. The individuals surrounding them return to their daily routines. Only then do patients comprehend the magnitude of their difficulties and that life is no longer the same. Many are overcome by sorrow, and everything seems unfamiliar. The gratitude wears off, and they start to feel very lonely.

Cancer treatment often takes a toll on the body, leaving it exhausted and weak. It can take a while for the body to adjust to this new normal, which can be discouraging for survivors.

Many may want to resume their old routines, but it can be disheartening when their body isn't ready or able to keep up. These limitations can lead to frustration and isolation.

Dealing with cancer can be highly isolating and burdensome, making it difficult to attend school, spend time with friends, or enjoy simple activities like running in the park or dancing in the rain. Time can stretch endlessly, much like the unattended flowers in a garden. Despite the love and support of family, the fear of the unknown can become overwhelming, and it may feel like your only solace is in the confines of your room.

Resisting the urge to let isolation take over your life is essential. If possible, utilize social media to stay connected with the world. Additionally, consider starting a journal to document your thoughts and feelings.

You could also draw pictures of the places you hope to visit and the adventures you plan to have when you recover. By keeping yourself occupied, you can avoid falling into a state of depression.

Transform your room into a garden of hope by adding colorful curtains, bright posters, and small throw rugs to liven up the place. Pull back the curtains to welcome the sunshine and open windows to listen to the birds. These kinds of actions help to create a haven of positivity in your environment, which will help lift your spirits during your treatments.

If you experience fatigue while receiving treatment, don't hesitate to ask for assistance and accept help from others. It's important to prioritize your tasks and take breaks to not push yourself too hard on good days. Plan activities when you feel your best and need to get things done.

As you go through your period of isolation, you may realize the importance of cherishing every moment and the strength you have found within yourself.

CHAPTER TWELVE

SURVIVORSHIP

"Life's better now. Maybe it was meant to happen for

many reasons because my life, in many ways, is richer."

—*Giuliana Rancic*

More people live longer with cancer thanks to early detection and new treatments. According to the National Cancer Institute (NCI), as of 2022, just over 18 million people in the United States are cancer survivors, meaning they have had or had cancer. Over the next ten years, experts anticipate a 24% increase in the number of people living with cancer.[1]

Cancer survivorship emphasizes cancer patients' health, well-being, and quality of life. It starts the day someone receives a cancer diagnosis, continues during and after treatment, and continues through the end of life.

Surviving cancer is an emotional journey that cannot be easily put into words. There is no set path, clear boundaries, or way to predict what will happen next. The experience of being a survivor can be just as challenging and exhausting as the actual cancer treatment, even if the toll is not as visible.

Survivorship for veterans with cancer extends beyond medical treatment. The brave individuals, who have already faced the rigors of combat, now confront a new battle against

---

[1] Surviving Cancer: Thriving During & After Treatment (clevelandclinic.org)

cancer, bringing its unique challenges, as the following three stories show.

I.   In his early twenties, a young and idealistic individual, Tommy Davis (name changed for privacy), felt a profound call to serve his country. He enlisted in the military, ready to defend the principles he believed in. With a deep sense of duty, he joined the ranks, full of hope and determination.

"As a veteran deployed to a conflict-ridden region, I witnessed the horrors of war firsthand. I faced enemy fire, experienced loss, and endured the emotional toll of seeing my comrades fall in battle. The war trauma left an indelible mark on my psyche, forever altering the course of my life.

"Upon returning home, I had to confront a new set of challenges. The physical and emotional wounds I carried weighed heavily on me, manifesting in symptoms of post-traumatic stress disorder (PTSD) and another formidable opponent: bladder cancer.

"For me, someone who was experiencing post-traumatic stress disorder (PTSD) from my time in service, a cancer diagnosis was complicated. It triggered traumatic memories and intensified my anxiety and depression. Additionally, my facing mortality from an enemy I could not see was very different from the life-threatening situations on the battlefield.

"The transition from the battlefield to civilian life proved arduous as I struggled to find a sense of purpose and belonging in a society unfamiliar with the realities of war. One of the most challenging aspects of survivorship for me was the isolation I felt.

"Despite the efforts of loved ones to understand and support me, I found it difficult to express the complexities of my experiences adequately. The divide between those who had served and those who had not created a barrier intensified my feelings of detachment and loneliness.

"Recognizing the need for assistance, I attended therapy sessions provided by veteran support organizations (DMV, AMVETS). These sessions allowed me to connect with fellow veterans who had undergone similar trials and understand their unique challenges. I found solace, camaraderie, and a newfound sense of belonging in these safe spaces.

"The camaraderie and support I received from fellow veterans played a pivotal role in my healing process. Through shared experiences and the knowledge that I was not alone, I began to embrace the strength within me to move forward.

"As I began to share my story, I realized the power of my voice in raising awareness about the difficulties veterans face after returning from war.

"Empowered by the community I had found, I immersed myself in advocacy work for fellow veterans. I

191

advocated for increased mental health support and resources for veterans with PTSD and other mental health issues.

"My determination to make a difference led me to connect with policymakers, veterans' organizations, and other stakeholders to push for legislative changes that would improve the lives of my comrades.

"Despite my countless challenges, I was honored to emerge as a beacon of hope for many. Through advocacy efforts and creating a support network for veterans, I proved that survivorship could lead to triumphs amidst trials. My story showcases the power of determination and the transformative impact of community support."

SURVIVORSHIP

The journey of survivorship for veterans is fraught with challenges, but it is also a testament to the resilience of the human spirit. Tommy Davis's story, one of millions, exemplifies the power of community, advocacy, and self-determination in overcoming the aftermath of war.

As a society, it is essential to recognize the sacrifices of our veterans and provide them with the support they need to heal and thrive. By doing so, we can honor their service and ensure that they find triumph amidst their trials.

Veterans diagnosed with cancer have already faced the rigors of combat and now confront a new battle against cancer, bringing its unique challenges beyond medical treatment, as the following brave individual demonstrates.

II.   Cancer, a relentless adversary, has the power to disrupt lives, sow seeds of despair, and impose unimaginable suffering. This story explores the profound journey of Jack bravely facing cancer, highlighting the emotional and physical toll of the disease while emphasizing the importance of compassion and support in such trying times.

"I'm Jack, and I've always been a fighter. From my days as a young recruit to my years as a seasoned veteran, I've faced challenges head-on with unwavering determination. But now, as I stare at the sterile hospital room around me, I meet a battle of a different kind – a fight against prostate cancer.

"The diagnosis hit me like a mortar shell, leaving me stunned, disorientated, and grappling with mixed emotions, fear, anger, and loneliness that I had never encountered on the battlefield.

"And as I lay in that hospital bed, I couldn't shake the feeling that this was a fight I might not be able to win, no matter how strong my will had been in the past.

"The room is silent, save for the steady beep of the heart monitor. My thoughts are a whirlwind of memories, fears, and regrets. I think back to comrades who had stood shoulder to shoulder with me in the line of fire.

"The faces of those I had lost over the years haunted me, their absence a stark reminder of the fragility of life.

"Without realizing it, I clench my fists, my knuckles turning white as I wrestle with my anger. "Why me?" "I was healthy one day, and suddenly, my good health evaporated like the morning dew.

"I was angry about my cancer and resented my healthcare providers, healthy friends, and loved ones. I even felt angry with God. I knew I was angry but didn't know how to deal with it other than suppressing it for fear of hurting someone. I didn't realize that squashing my anger caused fatigue, appetite loss, and low energy levels.

"I also felt a sense of sadness, which started me spiraling down into depression and loneliness. These feelings were exacerbated as family and friends struggled with my cancer diagnosis and didn't visit or call.

"I felt cut off and began to believe that no one cared, though some did but didn't know how. So, I stopped participating in the hobbies and activities I used to enjoy and didn't feel like reaching out. Even though people showed they cared about me, I felt no one understood my situation.

"The sense of helplessness gnawed at me, eroding the tough exterior I had built over decades. I had faced enemies in faraway lands, but this enemy was within, and it seemed to be winning the battle for my mind.

"It got so bad that one night, I found myself standing on the edge of the small lake on the hospital grounds, consumed by my inner demons. With tears streaming down my face, I contemplated ending my life, believing that my struggles had become insurmountable. Just as I was about to step forward, a faint voice called out from behind.

"It was Sarah, a nurse from the hospital who had been assisting me during treatment. She had sensed my growing desolation and had rushed to the lakeside in a desperate attempt to reach me. With empathy in her eyes, she shared her own experiences of witnessing the strength of patients who faced similar battles.

"Through our heartfelt conversations, I realized that my pain was not unique and that some people cared deeply for me. Sarah helped me understand that seeking help wasn't a sign of weakness but rather courage. She urged me to lean on my support network and to consider professional counseling to navigate my feelings.

"Over time, I started attending therapy sessions and opening up to my friends and family about my struggles. Their unwavering support began to mend the fractures in my spirit, and I gradually found a renewed sense of purpose.

"One day, as the sunlight filtered through the window, my grandson, Ethan, entered the room. The boy's youthful energy contrasted with the somber atmosphere that enveloped my hospital stay. Ethan had always admired my strength and bravery, often asking for stories about my time in the military.

'Hey, Grandpa,' Ethan said, a hint of concern in his voice as he saw the pain on my face.

'Hey, sport,' I replied, mustering a faint smile.

"Ethan pulled up a chair and sat beside my bed. 'You know, Grandpa, you've always been my hero. You're the bravest person I know.'

"I chuckled softly. 'Well, kid, being brave isn't always about charging into battle. Sometimes, it's about facing the things that scare you the most.'

"Ethan looked at me with wide eyes. 'Like fighting cancer?'

"I nodded, my gaze fixed on my grandson's earnest face. 'Exactly. It's a different battle, but I'm not giving up. Just like I never gave up on my comrades and country, I won't give up now.'

"Ethan's eyes sparkled with admiration. 'You've got this, Grandpa.'

"As the days turned into weeks, my perspective continued to shift. I realized that my experiences as a soldier had equipped me with a unique set of skills – resilience, adaptability, and a deep understanding of the value of camaraderie. I started to view my cancer diagnosis as another challenge to conquer, another enemy to face down.

"My fellow veterans rallied around me, offering encouragement and sharing stories of overcoming adversity. The bonds we had forged in battle proved decisive in the face of illness. And with each chemotherapy session and moment of uncertainty, I drew on my past to shape my present.

"Ethan continued to visit, bringing his vibrant spirit and a reminder that life was still moving forward. I shared my military service stories, imparting bravery and resilience lessons to my grandson. Our conversations became a source of strength for both of us, a reminder that the legacy of courage was being passed down through generations.

"The battle against cancer was far from easy. There were days of exhaustion and frustration, moments when doubt crept in. But I persevered with the support of my family, my fellow veterans, and the lessons I had learned on the battlefield. I faced the emotional rollercoaster with a newfound resolve, determined to emerge victorious again.

"In the end, my story becomes a testament to the fact that a warrior's spirit never truly fades. My emotional battle with cancer reminded me that bravery took on many forms and that the strength cultivated on the battlefield could carry one through even the most daunting challenges."

III.   Our final survivorship story takes place in a small town where a veteran named Samuel lives, who had seen his fair share of battles during his years of service. After returning home, he looked forward to a peaceful life, but fate had other plans.

He had faced the harshest battlefields and emerged with physical and emotional scars. But nothing could have prepared him for the news he received one cloudy afternoon – a liver cancer diagnosis.

"The news shook me to the core. I had already faced so much in life, and now this. I felt so angry, and I could feel it boiling inside me. I had always been faithful, trusting, and believing that God would care for me like He did when I was in the war.

"Me and God were tight, but when I started the treatments and the pain intensified, I questioned the fairness of it.

"As I struggled through chemotherapy sessions and grueling treatments, I couldn't understand why a life filled with hardship seemed to be my fate. My anger grew, and I felt abandoned by the God I had once turned to for guidance and strength.

"My wife, friends, and family tried to console me, encouraging me to lean on my faith during this difficult time. However, I couldn't shake the anger that had taken root in my heart. I distanced myself from my loved ones, retreating into a world of bitterness and despair.

"One day, as I sat alone in my backyard, I unleashed my pent-up anger toward the heavens. 'Why me, God, I cried out, demanding answers. I feel betrayed and hurt, and I want to know why I'm enduring such suffering after all I've been through.'

"Over time, my anger slowly became a quiet emptiness. I realized that my faith had sustained me through the most challenging times, and as I pushed it away, I felt even more lost. I had lost my health and my connection to something greater than myself.

"Early one morning, I sat in my favorite armchair, staring out the window as raindrops splattered against the glass. My hands trembled slightly, a stark contrast to the firm grip I had maintained on my rifle during my military days.

"The doctor's words echoed in my mind, mingling with memories of my past deployments. The feeling of vulnerability I had kept locked away for so long had come crashing back, just as formidable as the enemies I had once fought.

"I looked at the photographs on the mantelpiece – snapshots of my younger self in uniform, surrounded by comrades who had become like family. Each face held a story, a shared experience that was etched into the very core of my being.

"Tears welled in my eyes as I contemplated the possibility of leaving this world behind and saying goodbye to all I held dear.

"My wife, Elizabeth, entered the room and saw the distant look in my eyes. She had been my anchor through countless challenges, supporting me during my military service and the subsequent battles with post-traumatic stress. Now, facing the prospect of cancer, they were on the precipice of a new trial neither had anticipated.

"'Samuel,' she whispered, her voice a soothing balm. I turned to meet her gaze, and without a word, she knelt beside me, taking my trembling hands into her own. The touch of her warm skin grounded me, reminding me that I wasn't alone in this fight, just as I hadn't been alone on the battlefield.

"Tears streamed down my weathered cheeks as I finally released the stoicism that had defined my life. I shared my fears, regrets, and the overwhelming sense of injustice about confronting another battle. I spoke of the camaraderie I had felt in the military, the bonds that had sustained me, and the sorrow I felt over losing friends.

"My wife, Elizabeth, listened, her heart aching for the pain I was enduring. She held me close, allowing me to express my emotions without judgment. She didn't offer solutions or platitudes; she showed her presence, a safe space for me to grieve and confront my fears.

"Dawn turned into dusk, and my emotions flowed like the rain outside. I found solace in discussing my experiences as a soldier and a man grappling with my mortality. The weight of my burden lightened as I shared my innermost thoughts, allowing healing to take root in uncertainty.

"With my wife's unwavering support and willingness to embrace vulnerability, I began to see my diagnosis not as an insurmountable enemy but as another chapter in my journey. I realized that just as I had faced adversity, I could meet this new challenge with the same determination and resilience.

"That evening, the rain stopped as the sun set in a blaze of colors, I gazed at the rainbow on the horizon. The beauty of the world around me started to stir something within.

"Memories of my time in service, the camaraderie, and the sense of purpose reminded me that life was a mix of struggles and joys. While anger had consumed me for a while, I realized that moments of happiness and love still existed.

"With a heavy heart, I began to mend the bonds I had broken with my loved ones. Slowly, I started to rebuild my relationship with God as well. I understood my anger was a natural response to my circumstances, but I didn't want to let it define me."

Together, Samuel and Elizabeth embarked on a new battle – one against cancer. As they navigated the complexities of treatment and the rollercoaster of emotions, they did so hand in hand, drawing strength from the love they shared and the unbreakable bond they had forged over years of challenges.

As he continued his battle against cancer, Samuel found strength in reconnecting with his faith and those who cared about him. He learned that losing his faith temporarily was a part of his journey, and his struggles had the potential to reshape and deepen his beliefs.

Although Samuel had a tumultuous period of intense anger, he was able to use it as a catalyst for personal development, forgiveness, and rediscovery of his faith. His narrative showcases the incredible strength of the human spirit and the ability to heal, even in the face of significant trials.

Ultimately, his story symbolized the power of empathy, human connection, and the courage to confront and overcome our deepest emotions, regardless of how overwhelming they may seem. It's not simply a tale of a veteran's battle with cancer but a testament to the indomitable human spirit.

Cancer is a daunting opponent for veterans who have already endured the physical demands of military service. Their exposure to environmental hazards during service often intensifies the impact of cancer on their bodies.

Surviving cancer requires rigorous treatments such as surgery, chemotherapy, and radiation. However, these therapies take a toll on their bodies, leading to fatigue, pain, and potential long-term side effects.

Despite these challenges, veterans with cancer show unwavering strength, drawing on their military experience to persevere through the most challenging moments. They learn to adapt, embracing a new sense of self as they navigate physical changes and post-treatment rehabilitation.

The diagnosis can evoke traumatic memories worsen anxiety and depression, and confronting mortality can be particularly difficult for those who have already faced life-threatening situations on the battlefield.

Therefore, it is crucial to provide comprehensive emotional support for veterans with cancer throughout their journey as survivors. This involves integrating mental health care to promote resilience and lower the risk of developing chronic mental health problems.

During their journey as cancer survivors, veterans may face significant changes in their social life. They might find coping with their emotions and fears challenging, damaging their relationships with family and friends.

Additionally, they may feel disconnected and isolated from civilian life while undergoing cancer treatment, which makes accessing support networks difficult. To overcome these obstacles, support groups and peer counseling can effectively promote camaraderie and understanding among cancer veterans.

By sharing their experiences and finding common ground in military service and cancer survivorship, they can alleviate feelings of isolation and find a sense of community.

Receiving a cancer diagnosis can be a turning point for veterans, causing them to contemplate the significance of their lives. The awareness of their mortality may inspire them to find a new sense of purpose and a desire to contribute positively to their community.

Numerous veterans opt to give back by raising awareness for cancer and providing support, using their own experiences to assist others. This process of redefining their purpose can be a means of emotional recovery for veterans, enabling them to embrace survivorship as an occasion to create a lasting impact and benefit other survivors.

Offering improved support and advocacy for veterans who have survived cancer is crucial. Policymakers need to focus on enhancing access to top-notch healthcare, mental health services, and survivorship care that caters to the specific requirements of veterans. Healthcare providers should also undergo training to identify and tackle the challenges that veterans face during their journey.

By collaborating with veteran organizations, cancer institutes, and government bodies, a comprehensive approach to survivorship care can be ensured for these deserving individuals.

Surviving cancer as a veteran requires determination, bravery, and empathetic assistance. Despite enduring physical, emotional, and social obstacles, these veterans exhibit unwavering fortitude and leverage their military background to push through the most challenging moments.

By recognizing their distinct requirements, cultivating a sense of belonging, and promoting tailored support networks, we can guarantee their survival journey is met with the dignity and attention they merit.

Although I'm uncertain if time can heal all wounds, the passage of time gives us a chance to gain a different perspective and possibly discover a positive aspect of a negative situation. It helps us to find meaning within our struggles and difficulties.

It's important to realize that time can't make a cancer diagnosis disappear or eliminate the fear and agony that comes with it. Nonetheless, it allows us to accept our lives positive and negative aspects without regret.

Regardless of where you find yourself in your journey, remember that time can be a valuable tool for healing and growth, and you are not alone.

CONCLUSION

FROM DIAGNOSIS TO DEATH

"Our life doesn't end the minute we get

that diagnosis. We still have some living to do."

—Shannon Doherty

Cancer is a disease that affects people of all ages worldwide, and the news of its diagnosis can be devastating. According to the World Health Organization, cancer is responsible for one in six global deaths.

Studies show that one in three or even four out of ten people in the United States will eventually be diagnosed with cancer. Cancer can affect anyone in your personal or professional network.

Being diagnosed with cancer can be a challenging experience, and the road ahead can be overwhelming for patients and their loved ones as they face physical, emotional, and spiritual challenges.

The journey from diagnosis to the end of life can be lengthy and complicated, with many emotions and obstacles. It's common for patients and their families to feel shocked, scared, angry, and sad upon receiving the diagnosis, making it difficult to come to terms with the fact that their lives will be forever changed.

Dealing with cancer can not only affect your physical health, but it can also bring up a variety of unfamiliar emotions. These feelings can fluctuate throughout the day, hour, or even minute and intensify existing emotions.

Whether you are currently undergoing treatment, have completed treatment, or are a friend or family member, these emotions are entirely normal. How you deal with cancer may be influenced by the values you were raised with.

For example, some individuals may need to stay strong and protect their loved ones, while others may seek support from family, friends, or other cancer survivors.

Additionally, some may ask for help from professionals or counselors, while others may turn to their faith for comfort. It's important to remember that what works for one person may not work for another, so making decisions based on your needs and not comparing yourself to others is crucial.

It may also be helpful to confide in your loved ones if you feel comfortable doing so, as they may be experiencing similar emotions. Receiving a cancer diagnosis can make you feel like your life is spiraling out of control.

This can be due to uncertainty about your survival, disruptions to your daily routine due to doctor appointments and treatments, confusion from medical terminology, limitations on activities you once enjoyed, and feelings of helplessness and isolation. It's normal to experience these emotions, and it's essential to seek support during this difficult time.

If you're feeling overwhelmed, there are ways to regain control. Some people say that putting their lives in order helps. Being involved in your health care, asking questions, keeping your appointments, and changing your lifestyle are among the things you can control. Even setting a daily schedule can give you a sense of control.

While no one can control every thought, some say that they try not to dwell on the fearful ones but instead do what they can to enjoy the positive parts of life if they can, try to use their energy to focus on what makes you feel better and what you can do now to stay as healthy as possible.

Some people see their cancer as a "wake-up call." They realize the importance of enjoying the little things in life. They go places they've never been. They finish projects they had started but put them aside. They spend more time with friends and family. They mend broken relationships.

It may be hard at first, but look for joy if you have cancer. Pay attention to the things you do each day that make you smile. They can be as simple as drinking coffee, being with a child, or talking to a friend.

You can also do more unique things to you, like being in nature or praying in a place that has meaning. Or it could be playing a game you love or cooking a good meal. Whatever you choose, embrace the things that bring you joy when you can.

Developing a plan of care and educating yourself about your cancer can help make you feel more empowered. Don't hesitate to ask your doctor for more information and clarify any confusion.

It's okay to admit when you don't understand something. For some people, focusing on things other than cancer can feel better. If you desire, try participating in things you enjoy, such as music, crafts, reading, or learning something new.

Your care plan is the center of attention regarding surviving cancer. This plan typically covers details about the type of cancer you've been treated for, the treatments you've undergone, and recommendations for check-ups and follow-up tests. While survivorship care plans may vary, they usually include the following:

- **Your Check-up Schedule**

Your Check-Up Schedule may differ depending on your circumstances. Individuals usually see their healthcare team every three to four months during the initial years following treatment and less frequently afterward. Nevertheless, getting in touch with your healthcare provider immediately is crucial if you observe any changes in your body.

- **Testing**

During your check-ups, you may need to undergo blood and imaging tests. Not all cancer types and treatments may cause late effects, and the kind of late effects can vary depending on your situation. Therefore, inform your healthcare provider of any changes in your family medical history or new supplements you're taking.

- **Your Care Plan**

Your survivorship care plan may contain advice on healthy eating habits and exercises. Additionally, it might offer information on national and regional support groups where you can connect with other cancer survivors.

After cancer treatment, some individuals may not require regular checkups and follow-up tests, and they might thrive in their post-treatment life. However, those with ongoing, second, or advanced cancers need continuous medical follow-up and various survivorship support.

- **Lifestyle changes**

Risk factors refer to activities and lifestyle choices that increase your chances of developing cancer. You can reduce your risk of developing recurring or second cancers by making lifestyle changes. If you smoke, it's advisable to stop. Giving up tobacco and avoiding second-hand smoke can improve your overall health.

It's crucial to understand that consuming alcohol may heighten the chances of developing different types of cancer. It's advisable to limit or completely stop drinking alcohol if possible.

Sun exposure can lead to skin cancer, so everyone must protect themselves. If you're taking medications that make you more vulnerable to the sun, consult your healthcare provider to select the best sunscreen and other ways to keep your skin safe.

Maintaining a healthy diet after cancer treatment is crucial, and food safety should be given priority. Specific cancer treatments may affect the immune system, increasing the risk of food poisoning. Some individuals may have difficulty eating after treatment, so it's recommended to consult with a dietitian to discuss concerns and alternative food options.

Regular exercise offers many benefits, such as managing anxiety and depression, enhancing strength and endurance, and boosting self-confidence. However, before starting a new exercise routine, it's best to consult with your healthcare provider. They can provide personalized recommendations and ensure that you don't risk injury.

Cancer can significantly impact those it affects, but cancer survivorship can help individuals adapt to these changes. The focus is on maintaining good health and wellness from diagnosis to the end of life, allowing cancer patients to maintain a high quality of life.

Healthcare providers understand how cancer can alter one's life and create a personalized survivorship plan to account for any changes. They are also there to support patients throughout their journey.

Some individuals feel relief upon completing cancer treatment, but others have grown accustomed to their routine and interacting with healthcare providers. They may feel lost without this familiarity. It is common for cancer patients and their loved ones to believe that the end of treatment signifies the end of cancer-related worries and the desire to return to pre-cancer routines.

Research shows that cancer survivors may struggle to recover physically, emotionally, psychologically, and socially. Some may even develop post-traumatic stress disorder related to their diagnosis.

The journey of battling cancer can be exhausting. Once treatment is over, individuals strive to return to their daily lives. However, the fear of cancer recurrence can impede their progress.

Many cancer survivors often experience anxiety about the possibility of cancer recurrence. It's natural for them to want to eliminate this fear to improve their quality of life. However, simply suggesting that they "stay positive" may not help ease their worries.

Recovering after cancer treatment can be a difficult journey. While some survivors may find ways to reconnect with their goals, others may need to adjust or abandon specific goals altogether. This process can be painful and requires time to work through.

Feeling vulnerable when making plans or having hopes is normal, especially after experiencing disappointment. It's understandable to worry about it happening again. However, the fragility of our goals has always been present, even if we may have just realized it.

It's okay to feel lost even if you've followed all the recommendations, as there's no guarantee that the issue won't resurface. It can be demoralizing to be derailed from important aspects of your life, like education, family, work, or other responsibilities.

When dealing with anxiety related to cancer recurrence, it's common to experience a range of emotions. For instance, individuals may feel angry about their diagnosis because they believe they did everything right but still ended up with cancer.

This can create confusion and helplessness about protecting oneself from cancer. Identifying these emotions is the first step in managing cancer anxiety. It's equally important to identify external factors that trigger anxiety.

For example, while awareness campaigns for cancer can promote the importance of screening, they can also inundate individuals with constant reminders about the disease, which can have positive and negative effects.

During Breast Cancer Awareness Month in October, pink ribbons are everywhere, which can overwhelm many people. While some may find the display of pink ribbons empowering, others may find it to be a painful reminder of their past struggles and an uncertain future.

Cancer is frequently discussed on television, whether it be a public service announcement encouraging the use of HPV vaccines, a news report on the latest scientific findings, or an episode of a medical drama.

When we hear about other people's struggles, we often empathize with them, even if we don't know them personally. However, it's important to remember that hearing about other people's experiences with cancer can also trigger traumatic memories for some individuals.

Gaining knowledge is essential, especially when faced with uncertainty. However, excessive searching for symptoms and statistics can lead to overwhelming anxiety-inducing information.

Experts recommend a three-step "information hygiene" process for accurate information gathering. Step one is to formulate a specific question. Step two involves limiting your search to trustworthy sources that can answer your question. Finally, taking a break from technology is important to digest the information gathered.

Individuals who have experienced cancer tend to be highly in tune with their bodies, while those with anxiety often experience physical manifestations of stress. It can be challenging for people with minimal or no symptoms to differentiate between momentary physical sensations and indications that require medical attention.

The inability to eliminate anxiety can exacerbate the issue, leading to intensified fear of recurrence and progression. Without adequate coping strategies, this fear can become unmanageable.

In the end stages of the disease, patients may require more intensive care as they experience a deterioration in physical and cognitive abilities. As the end nears, patients may face various symptoms, including changes in breathing, reduced consciousness, and pain.

Patients and their families must know what to expect during this time, and healthcare providers can ensure that the patient is comfortable and pain-free.

It's important to remember that hope and love can still be found during the dying process. Patients and their families can find comfort in spiritual practices like prayer, meditation, and the love and support of those around them.

Hospice and palliative care can also provide comfort and support, helping patients maintain their dignity and quality of life until the end. Though the journey from diagnosis to the end of life can be challenging, patients and their families are not alone.

Healthcare providers, loved ones, and spiritual practices can all offer comfort, strength, and peace during this difficult time.

AFTERWORD

The First 72 Hours - A Guide After a Cancer Loss

"The song is ended but the melody lingers on."

Irving Berlin

The first 72 hours after losing a loved one to cancer can be overwhelming. Emotions are many, and finding the right way or place to grieve can be challenging. Receiving genuine support, empathy, and practical assistance can make a significant difference during this delicate time. In this summation, we will revisit meaningful ways to obtain comfort and aid within hours after a cancer-related death. Angee Costa Learned that all too well after the death of her friend.

"She's with God."

"That was the text message that appeared on my phone's screen one morning. In that moment, time stood still. Nothing existed. The whole world went blank as if the whiteboard of life had been completely erased and the universe ceased to be. As I stood there frozen for several seconds, time started to move forward again and the world was recreated around me. But it was a world without Mel — a completely different world, absent of her fire, wit, humor, and sheer brilliance.

"I had been begging Mel to write her novel and start her memoirs business for almost a year. She was one of the greatest minds I have ever known and, together, I thought we would be a force to be reckoned with. Finally, over the summer, we got her book done. She was so proud when it became a best seller, we got busy working on book two. But before we could finish and long before we could lay the plan of our business partnership, the text message came:

She's with God.

"I don't know what people mean when they talk about stages of grief. I didn't go through stages. They all came rushing at me at once. I wanted to fall to the floor while kicking and screaming while punching the wall while shaking fists at the heavens while accepting that I knew this day would come. I couldn't even cry. Tears seemed woefully inefficient to express the cacophony of emotions coursing through me.

"I felt I had been cheated somehow — as if life wasn't fair. Evidence? Well, first of all, it wasn't fair that it was Mel. She had been through so much. A troubled relationship with her mother, difficulty with her family, a tragic divorce, a nasty financial battle, and the death of her granddaughter at a young age. I felt she had been dealt enough blows and deserved a break. Why would she have to die?

"Number Two. Mel was everything: mother, teacher, preacher, community leader, author, playwright, entrepreneur, singer, coach. She was one of those people everybody should get to meet. You were never the same after an encounter with her. Unique... distinct from any other human being. From her wise-cracking wit to her brightly colored hair, she was always a delightful surprise. She was a no-nonsense gal, not one of those people whose opinions are obscure. She didn't mind putting you in your place when you needed it. And I loved her for it. To bury all of that talent in a grave seemed like the most absurd thing I'd ever heard.

"Number Three. I had just talked to her. Of course, that's what people say when someone they love dies. But I <u>had</u> just talked to her. She had been diagnosed with cancer a year earlier. And, despite my ridiculously packed schedule, I always made time to talk to her when she called. A conversation with Mel was an hour if it was a minute. It took at least an hour to experience all of the enchantment she had to offer. She would teach, entertain, scold, enlighten, and spill the tea on anybody who wasn't measuring up to their potential — starting with herself. In our last conversation, we philosophized, we cried, we debated, we consulted. We solved all the world's problems in that call! And we laughed. We always, always laughed. That was the magic of Mel. She never left you without a reason to bend over in a gut-busting belly laugh.

"Number Four. I thought sick people were supposed to wither away. I thought they were supposed to slowly sink into the depths of their illness until they were gone. But she didn't. Or, if she did, she didn't let me know. I was, after all, 1500 miles away. She could have easily shielded me from the present and coming truths. But that day... that day I talked to her, she was the same spitfire I had always known. Alert, intense, engaging, and fun.

"There are a thousand more reasons why I feel her death was not fair. But one thing is clear: I don't have the power to change anything about it. All I have left now are the memories. Memories... and questions:

- "Why is cancer still an issue in this world of modern technology and medical advancements? What will it take to solve it? Why can't we just stop everything and put all the greatest minds on this one problem? Naïve, I know.

- "What should I be doing in these moments just after her death? How do I prioritize my own grief with the mourning and immediate needs of the family, especially her son who is so special to me?

- "What is appropriate to ask? Since I spoke to her just before she died, is it rude to ask what happened or how it happened?

- "How do I properly support her family in the days to come? What's the right amount of phone calls, text messages?

234

Are text messages too impersonal? Should I drop family and business, jump on a plane, and get there now?

• "How do I preserve her legacy appropriately? I want to do something, but I don't know what to do.

"There will be long days ahead. Perhaps I'll find answers to all of my questions. And perhaps there are some questions that have no answers on this side of heaven. This I know: I was blessed with the most wonderful friend. And no matter what the future holds, she shines so brightly in my heart, I will never forget her."

MOVING FORWARD

Losing a loved one can be an extremely difficult experience, and it's crucial to receive support from others who are compassionate and understanding. When someone close to us passes away, it's natural to feel unsure about what to do next.

However, it's important to remember that we need support now more than ever. We don't need a specific plan; having someone present can provide immense comfort. Whether they offer their physical, virtual, or telephonic presence, allowing them to be there for us as a supportive companion is helpful.

Going through a grieving process can be very difficult. However, having someone there to support and care for us can help us cope with the pain and gradually begin to heal. It's common to experience depression, anger, guilt, and sadness when grieving. We may feel isolated and alone in our grief, but reaching out to someone can make a world of difference.

We must not let our discomfort prevent us from seeking help. Even if we're not ready to talk about our feelings, their presence can be comforting, and their support can help us deal with our emotions.

When we seek grief support, the person offering the support will follow our lead by being present and listening to us compassionately. They understand that everyone grieves differently, and it's important for them not to impose their expectations on us during our journey.

They know to respect our unique way of coping with our loss, whether it involves shedding tears, expressing anger, or even finding moments of laughter as we reminisce about our loved ones. Their presence and listening can be a massive source of comfort and healing, allowing us to express our feelings and memories, which can immensely help.

Our grief support will consider our cultural and religious practices and align them with our beliefs. People can offer comfort and support such as "I'm so sorry for your loss" or "My heart goes out to you during this difficult time."

Additionally, they will provide practical assistance by helping with grocery shopping, arranging funerals, cleaning, making phone calls, or coordinating meals for the family.

In the initial 72 hours following a loss, even small acts of kindness can significantly ease the burden of grief. When we seek support, we can receive the help we need. It's important to remind ourselves to take care of our own well-being by taking a short walk, having a nutritious meal, or getting rest.

Accepting the support and presence of empathetic individuals who are willing to help us can provide us with the much-needed comfort and strength to navigate the difficult journey of grief.

:

APPENDIX A

NOURISHING HOPE

"When Diet Is Wrong, Medicine Is of No Use.
When Diet Is Correct, Medicine Is of No Need."
—*Ayurvedic Proverb*

The process of battling cancer can be a challenging physical and mental journey. A cancer diagnosis is a life-altering event that prompts individuals to reassess many aspects of their lifestyle, including their diet.

Recently, the importance of a healthy diet in supporting cancer treatment and recovery has gained significant recognition. While diet alone cannot cure cancer, it plays a significant role in supporting treatment, managing side effects, and promoting overall well-being.

Oncology dieticians guide patients toward dietary choices that positively impact their treatment outcomes and overall well-being.

In this appendix, we explored the efforts of an oncology dietitian in encouraging a healthy diet for a veteran diagnosed with cancer while highlighting the importance of their role in the patient's journey to recovery.

In a quiet corner of the bustling VA hospital, a veteran named Robert sat, grappling with the weight of a recent cancer diagnosis. As he stared out the window, lost in thought, a warm, compassionate voice brought him back to the present.

"Hello, Robert. My name is Sarah, and I'm an oncology dietitian. I'm here to provide information and support to help you navigate this journey."

With a kind smile, Sarah sat beside Robert, understanding the overwhelming emotions he must be experiencing. She began by explaining the role of nutrition in cancer treatment and recovery.

She shared stories of other patients she had worked with, emphasizing how a well-balanced diet had helped them manage treatment side effects, maintain energy levels, and improve overall well-being.

Listening attentively, Robert felt a glimmer of hope. For the first time since his diagnosis, he saw a way to contribute to his healing actively.

Sarah's patience was remarkable as she offered explanations to help him understand how certain nutrients could strengthen his immune system and support his body during the challenges ahead.

Sarah delved into Robert's dietary habits and preferences as the conversation continued. She recognized the importance of meeting him where he was, understanding that drastic changes might be overwhelming. Together, they discussed his favorite foods and ways to incorporate healthier choices without feeling deprived.

Her expertise shone as she addressed the potential side effects of treatment. She offered practical tips to combat nausea, suggested small, frequent meals to manage fatigue, and recommended hydration strategies to counteract dehydration. With each piece of advice, Robert felt more equipped to face the journey ahead.

What truly set Sarah apart was her genuine care and emotional support. She acknowledged the diagnosis's emotional toll and its impact on eating habits. She shared stories of resilience, reminding Robert that he was not alone in his struggle. Her encouragement ignited a sense of determination within him.

Over the next few weeks, Sarah remained a steady presence in Robert's life. She provided him with easy-to-follow recipes aligned with his treatment plan and dietary requirements.

She checked in regularly, discussing his challenges and adjusting the nutrition plan. Her unwavering support gave Robert the confidence to make healthier choices and prioritize his well-being.

As treatment progressed, Robert began to experience positive changes. He found himself more energetic and better able to cope with the side effects. His outlook on his journey shifted from one of fear to one of empowerment.

Sarah's guidance had not only improved his physical health but had also infused him with a newfound sense of hope.

One day, after a successful treatment session, Robert looked out the window again. This time, he saw the world with renewed optimism. The support he received from Sarah illuminated his path through the darkness of diagnosis and treatment.

With her guidance, Robert realized that nourishing his body was a means of survival, just as nurturing his spirit was essential for reclaiming control over his life.

Sarah's expertise, empathy, and unwavering support ultimately transformed Robert's cancer journey. She proved that a dietitian's role extends beyond just providing nutritional advice – it encompasses uplifting spirits, fostering resilience, and nourishing hope in the face of adversity.

After the diagnosis, the oncology dietitian plays a pivotal role, explaining the significance of providing customized nutritional guidance to the veteran. Every veteran's health condition, treatment plan, and food choices differ, and the dietitian invests time in comprehending the veteran's medical history, treatment schedule, and current dietary routine. This approach creates a tailored nutrition plan to supplement the veteran's cancer treatment.

The dietitian approaches the veteran with an educational mindset, educating them on the impact of a healthy diet on their journey. They discuss the benefits of certain nutrients in boosting the immune system, increasing energy levels, and reducing treatment-related side effects.

The veteran is empowered to make informed dietary choices through scientific explanations and tangible benefits.

When undergoing chemotherapy and radiation, it's common to experience side effects like nausea, fatigue, and changes in taste. To help with these challenges, a dietitian provides helpful tips to alleviate the impact on a veteran's diet.

This includes suggestions for easy-to-digest foods, hydration advice, and flavor-enhancing techniques to ensure the veteran maintains proper nutrition despite any difficulties.

The dietitian knows sticking to a healthy diet can be emotionally challenging, particularly for cancer patients. To help the veteran, they offer ongoing encouragement and emotional support, emphasizing the positive effects of healthy dietary choices on their well-being.

This support is vital in keeping the veteran motivated and committed to healthier food choices.

Throughout the veteran's treatment journey, the oncology dietitian remains highly involved. They consistently check the veteran's nutritional status, evaluate any shifts in dietary preferences or needs, and adjust the nutrition plan accordingly.

This flexibility guarantees that the veteran's diet matches their ever-changing health demands. The dietitian's dedication to promoting a healthy diet for a veteran diagnosed with cancer highlights their commitment to providing comprehensive patient care.

They provide personalized guidance, education, and emotional support while addressing treatment-related challenges and continuously monitor the patient's progress.

By recognizing each patient's individuality and fostering a collaborative approach, oncology dietitians empower veterans to take an active role in their healing journey. Such initiatives are a testament to the holistic approach that modern oncology embraces as the medical community continues to explore the complex link between diet and cancer outcomes.

The following list explores some of the best dietary practices for cancer patients, considering the disease's complexity and the various treatment stages.

Nutrient-Dense Foods

A diet rich in nutrient-dense foods can provide essential vitamins, minerals, antioxidants, and other bioactive compounds that support the body's immune system and help mitigate treatment-related side effects.

Incorporating various colorful fruits and vegetables, whole grains, lean proteins, and healthy fats can offer the necessary nutrients for optimal health.

Balanced Macronutrients

Maintaining a balanced intake of macronutrients—carbohydrates, proteins, and fats—is crucial. Carbohydrates provide energy, while proteins support tissue repair and immune function. Healthy fats, such as those in nuts, seeds, and fatty fish, contribute to overall well-being.

Hydration

Staying adequately hydrated is essential, as cancer treatments and medications can lead to dehydration. Drinking water, herbal teas, and hydrating foods like fruits and vegetables can help manage this concern.

Anti-Inflammatory Foods

An anti-inflammatory diet rich in berries, turmeric, ginger, and leafy greens may help reduce chronic inflammation linked to cancer development and progression. Minimizing processed foods, sugary snacks, and excessive red meat consumption can support an anti-inflammatory approach.

Individualization

Cancer is a complex disease with many variations, and each person's nutritional needs can differ based on cancer type, treatment plan, overall health, and personal preferences.

Consulting a registered dietitian with experience in oncology can help tailor a diet to an individual's specific needs.

Managing Side Effects

Cancer treatments often lead to side effects like nausea, fatigue, and loss of appetite. Eating small, frequent meals, avoiding bland and easy-to-digest foods, and considering nutritional supplements if necessary can help manage these challenges.

Avoiding Extreme Diets

While specific diets claim to cure cancer, extreme dietary restrictions can do more harm than good by depriving the body of essential nutrients. It's crucial to approach dietary changes with caution and under the guidance of medical professionals.

Emotional and Mental Well-being

Cancer takes a toll not only physically but also emotionally and mentally. A supportive diet that includes foods rich in omega-3 fatty acids (found in fatty fish and flaxseeds) can potentially support cognitive function and emotional well-being.

A cancer diagnosis necessitates a holistic approach to health, where diet plays a crucial role. While there is no one-size-fits-all answer to the best diet for individuals diagnosed with cancer, focusing on nutrient-dense foods, balanced macronutrients, hydration, and individualization can contribute to better treatment outcomes, improved quality of life, and overall well-being.

Working closely with healthcare professionals, including oncologists and registered dietitians, is important to develop a personalized dietary plan that supports your unique journey through cancer treatment and recovery.

APPENDIX B

CAREGIVER SUPPORT

"Caregiving is a constant learning experience."

—Vivian Frazier

Once upon a time, in a quiet suburban neighborhood, lived Sarah and David, a couple who had weathered the storms of life together. David, a proud veteran, had served his country with honor, but life was about to present them with their greatest challenge yet.

One sunny afternoon, the doctor's office delivered a devastating blow: "David, your test results came back, and you have prostate cancer." The news shook their world, leaving them both scared and uncertain about what lay ahead.

This was not what they were expecting as they advanced in life. But amid this adversity, Sarah decided to become David's caregiver, just as he had always been her rock.

The journey towards cancer treatment was marked by a flurry of doctor's appointments, tests, and treatments. Sarah played the role of advocate and caregiver with unwavering determination.

She researched treatment options, attended every appointment with the doctor, and asked questions until she understood David's condition.

As David underwent his treatments, Sarah's responsibilities expanded. She became proficient in administering medications and offering emotional support during challenging moments. Their connection deepened as they overcame each obstacle together.

Although there were times of frustration and hopelessness, they tackled them as a team, with their love and dedication shining brightly.

The couple received support from their loved ones through a difficult time. Friends and family provided meals, assistance with household tasks, and emotional comfort. Sarah's sister, Emily, cared for David occasionally, giving Sarah the chance to rest and focus on her health. She needed to maintain her strength for both David and her.

As the weeks passed, they turned into months, and although the fight against cancer was tough, there were still moments of happiness and optimism. David's determination and Sarah's constant encouragement were a source of inspiration for everyone.

They found comfort in the little moments they shared, like exchanging smiles during chemotherapy, embracing each other after a difficult night, and enjoying a home-cooked meal together.

Despite the uncertainty that cancer brought into their lives, Sarah and David lived each day to the fullest. They celebrated anniversaries, birthdays, and even quiet moments of togetherness. Their love remained unshaken, a testament to the strength of their bond.

One bright morning, the doctor delivered the long-awaited news that David was in remission. The heavy burden weighing on their hearts was lifted, and tears of happiness streamed down their faces. Although the journey had been burdensome, their love had remained steadfast.

As they walked hand in hand out of the hospital that day, Sarah knew their journey was far from over. The physical and emotional scars would remain, but they had faced the darkest times together and emerged stronger.

Their love, tested by the trials of cancer, had proven unbreakable. Sarah, the devoted wife of a veteran and an unwavering caregiver had shown that love could conquer even the greatest of challenges.

The role of a caregiver for a veteran diagnosed with cancer is paramount, as it involves addressing the physical aspects of the disease and providing emotional and psychological support to the individual who has dedicated their life to serving their country.

Caregivers shoulder immense responsibilities, from ensuring the veteran's physical well-being to offering companionship and understanding during trying times. This Appendix investigates caregivers' multifaceted roles and significant responsibilities in supporting veterans facing cancer.

Physical Care

Caregivers play a crucial role in managing the veteran's physical health. This includes administering medications, assisting with mobility, arranging medical appointments, and caring for treatment regimens. Cancer treatments can often be demanding, and caregivers ensure that the veteran's health needs are met effectively.

Emotional Support

A cancer diagnosis can trigger various emotions, including fear, anxiety, and depression. Caregivers provide a stable emotional anchor, offering reassurance, empathy, and a listening ear. They create a safe space for veterans to express their feelings without judgment, helping them navigate the emotional challenges that arise during their cancer journey.

Advocacy

Navigating the healthcare system can be overwhelming, especially for veterans who may already be dealing with service-related health issues. Caregivers step into the role of advocates, ensuring that the veteran receives the best possible care. They communicate with medical professionals, coordinate appointments, and ensure the veteran's preferences and concerns are considered.

Practical Assistance

Caregivers assist with daily activities that the veteran might find challenging due to their health condition. This includes meal preparation, housekeeping, transportation, and personal care. By helping with these tasks, caregivers alleviate some of the burdens associated with the veteran's illness, allowing them to focus on their recovery.

Companionship

Cancer treatment can often lead to isolation, as veterans may be unable to engage in their usual social activities. Caregivers provide companionship and prevent feelings of loneliness. They engage in conversations, hobbies, and activities that bring joy and a sense of normalcy to the veteran's life.

Communication and Information

Caregivers act as a bridge between the veteran and the medical team. They ensure the veteran understands their diagnosis, treatment options, and potential side effects. Caregivers also help veterans make informed decisions about their healthcare by gathering relevant information and presenting it understandably.

End-of-Life Care

In cases where cancer becomes terminal, caregivers play a crucial role in ensuring that the veteran's final days are as comfortable and dignified as possible. They offer emotional support to the veteran and their family, help with pain management, and ensure their wishes are respected.

CARE FOR THE CAREGIVER

As the caregiver for your cancer patient, you have a crucial role to play in their well-being. Your responsibilities go beyond just medical care, and you are there to offer emotional, physical, and psychological support to them.

Your commitment, compassion, and advocacy are essential to their recovery and reflect the gratitude and respect they deserve for their service to the nation.

We appreciate your dedication to this crucial role, but it's essential to acknowledge the steps needed to maintain your health while providing care. Caregiving can be physically and emotionally draining, so you must prioritize self-care to offer the best support.

Caring for your cancer patient is an immense responsibility, and your well-being is often overlooked. Your role can be emotionally, physically, and mentally taxing, leading to burnout and stress. Recognizing and addressing your needs is essential to ensure that you can continue providing adequate support to your veteran loved ones.

We acknowledge the importance of caring for the caregivers of patients diagnosed with cancer and explore strategies to offer you the support you deserve.

As a caregiver, you may encounter a range of unique challenges. It would be best if you navigated the complexities of cancer care while managing the emotional impact of your loved one's service and diagnosis.

These challenges can lead to chronic stress, anxiety, and even depression. It's important to prioritize self-care, as your well-being has a direct impact on the quality of care you're able to provide.

If you become overwhelmed, you may not be able to offer adequate support, which could adversely affect your patient's overall health outcomes. By prioritizing your well-being and taking care of yourself, you can ensure you can provide the best care for your patient.

Most caregivers often neglect their physical health while tending to their patient's loved ones. Prioritizing your health through regular exercise, balanced nutrition, and sufficient rest is essential. This benefits your well-being and equips you to provide better care.

Emotional Support

You need to have a secure place where you can freely express your emotions and feelings. You may benefit from counseling, support groups, or open discussions with friends and family about your worries, fears, and frustrations. These resources can help you handle your responsibilities more effectively.

Respite Care

You must also take regular breaks to avoid burnout. Respite care allows you to take time off, participate in activities you enjoy, and recharge. Temporary relief can be provided by family members, friends, or professional respite services.

Education and Training

Learning new skills to manage your patient's medical needs may sometimes be necessary. Access to proper training and resources can increase your confidence and decrease stress. This may involve learning about cancer treatments, managing medications, and identifying symptoms.

Community and Social Support

Building a community of fellow caregivers can provide a strong support system. Sharing experiences, advice, and coping strategies can alleviate feelings of isolation and give you a sense of belonging.

Mental Health Services

You may experience heightened levels of stress, anxiety, or depression. Access to mental health services can equip you with coping mechanisms and strategies to manage your emotional well-being.

Conclusion

Taking care of the caregiver of a patient diagnosed with cancer is crucial, not only as an act of compassion but also as a necessity. The well-being of their caregivers directly influences the patient's quality of care.

Providing emotional support, respite care, education, and community connections can help caregivers develop resilience and compassion and continue their invaluable role. As a society, we must recognize caregivers' sacrifices and ensure they receive the care and support they deserve.

APPENDIX C

SPIRITUAL CARE

"Keep your faith to God, to your family, and to yourself. There is no other better way to fight cancer when you know that there are lives around you that fight beside you."

—*Aaron Simmons*

Spirituality is a difficult concept as it is highly personal and varies from individual to individual. For some, spirituality is expressed through religious practices and beliefs, while for others, it may be expressed through a connection to nature, music, or art.

Spiritual support does not necessarily mean providing religious support but acknowledging the patient's spiritual beliefs and values and incorporating them into their care.

For veteran oncology patients, spiritual support can be critical as they face a life-threatening illness. They may question their purpose in life, struggle with feelings of isolation, and may experience a loss of hope.

Spiritual care can help them find meaning and purpose in their lives, even in the face of illness. It can also give them a sense of community and connection with others with similar beliefs and values.

Spiritual care can take many forms, including prayer, meditation, counseling, and support groups. Chaplains and other spiritual care providers are often available in VA hospitals and community care centers to support veteran patients and their families.

These providers can assist veterans in exploring their spiritual beliefs, provide comfort, and assist in helping them find meaning and purpose in their lives.

Research has shown that spiritual support can positively impact oncology patients' physical and emotional well-being. Studies have found that veteran patients who receive spiritual support have fewer symptoms of depression and anxiety, experience less pain, and have a better quality of life.

Spiritual support has also been shown to improve veteran patient satisfaction with their care and their ability to cope with their illness.

Spiritual support is an essential aspect of care for oncology veteran patients. It can provide them with comfort, hope, and meaning and assist them in coping with their illness's emotional and spiritual aspects.

Medical treatments and therapies are important, but addressing veterans' emotional and spiritual needs is equally important in providing comprehensive care. Healthcare providers should acknowledge the importance of spiritual support and work to integrate it into the care of oncology patients.

Cancer can be a challenging physical and emotional experience, and incorporating spiritual practices can benefit many people. Here are some spiritual practices that may be included in a curriculum for cancer care:

1. **Meditation:** Meditation is a practice that involves training the mind to focus and become more aware of the present moment. It can help to reduce stress, decrease anxiety, and improve overall well-being.

2. **Prayer:** Prayer is a practice that involves communicating with a higher power and can be a source of comfort and strength for many people. It can provide a sense of connection

to something greater than oneself and help cultivate feelings of hope and faith.

3. **Gratitude:** Cultivating a sense of gratitude involves focusing on the positive aspects of life, even during challenging times. This can involve consciously noticing and appreciating the small things, such as a beautiful sunset or a kind gesture from a loved one.

4. **Forgiveness:** Forgiveness is a practice that involves letting go of anger and resentment towards oneself or others. It can be a difficult practice but can help to promote healing and inner peace.

5. **Connection with nature:** Spending time in nature can help to promote feelings of calmness and inner peace. This can involve taking walks in the heart, spending time in a garden, or simply spending time outside and appreciating the beauty of the natural world.

6. **Mindfulness:** Mindfulness is a practice that involves being fully present in the moment without judgment or distraction. It can help promote calmness and inner peace and be a valuable tool for managing stress and anxiety.

7. **Creative expression:** Engaging in creative activities, such as writing, painting, or music, can help to promote feelings of joy and self-expression. This can be a valuable tool for coping with the emotional challenges of cancer.

Incorporating spiritual practices into cancer care can be a valuable tool for promoting healing and inner peace. It is important to remember that each person's spiritual journey is unique, and what works for one person may not work for another.

Therefore, working with a qualified healthcare provider to develop a spiritual curriculum tailored to individual needs and preferences is important.

As clinical chaplains and spiritual care advisors, we work with patients to assess their spiritual needs, explore their meaning and purpose, and determine if they have a faith community or support system.

We respect the patient's faith, culture, beliefs, and traditions concerning their lives sacred, existential, emotional, and spiritual aspects. Being present and emotionally connected to the patient creates a safe space for them to share their concerns and pain.

When working with cancer patients, we focus on the patient and their current situation, whether it's a diagnosis, survivorship, or the news that their cancer cannot be treated. We conduct a spiritual assessment before chemotherapy to determine what may contribute to their stress and suffering.

As we are more involved in the patient's internal struggles, we aim to rekindle their faith and provide ways to use their beliefs to cope with their situation. We aim to help the patient reflect on their loss of identity, the pain of receiving a diagnosis, the fear of abandonment, and the belief that their prayers are not working.

We understand that this deep, unseen pain is often caused by unforgiveness and regret and cannot be addressed with a stethoscope or scalpel. We act like skilled horticulturists, cultivating the soil of the soul, removing anything that impedes growth, and planting seeds of inspiration that encourage new beginnings - things that nourish spiritual and emotional health.

We ask open-ended questions to assess the patient's spiritual health and practical resources, such as "What gives you meaning and purpose right now?" and "Who or what do you need to forgive?"

We develop a spiritual care plan that addresses their inner spiritual pain and needs to assist in their healing. We focus on the three everyday spiritual needs: love and connection, meaning and purpose, and forgiveness.

We investigate these needs to understand the patient's spirituality and their existing rituals and practices. We ensure the patient has a religious community that affirms their value and offers compassionate support.

We determine if there are individuals who can provide practical support, such as home visits for errands or transportation, or uplift with prayer.

It has become increasingly evident that providing spiritual support to cancer patients is paramount. Therefore, healthcare professionals, particularly Chaplains, should assess the spiritual requirements of patients and create and administer culturally appropriate spiritual care.

Chaplains, nurses, and healthcare providers must acknowledge the influence of spirituality and cultural aspects on the health of cancer patients and address any impediments

to delivering extensive and appropriate care to each patient.

ABOUT THE AUTHOR

Dr. Larry D. Black is a retired Navy and VA chaplain who founded and runs TALL & Associates LLC. This firm offers counseling, coaching, and consulting services for leaders and aspiring leaders. Dr. Black's extensive military background and Doctorate in leadership give him a deep understanding of leadership theory, organizational dynamics, and the challenges of leading in diverse and rapidly changing environments. Dr. Black's passion for leadership is evident in his ability to inspire and innovate, making him a valuable resource for anyone looking to improve their leadership skills.

Dr. Black is a Board-Certified chaplain specializing in Hospice/Palliative Care and Grief Recovery. He uses evidence-based Biblical principles to help veterans and civilians strengthen their relationship with God, unite, and serve Christ's mission in the world. Dr. Black has successfully implemented transformative programs locally and globally, benefiting thousands of civilians, military personnel, and veterans struggling with emotional and spiritual issues. If you want to improve your leadership skills with a strong sense of discipline, teamwork, and adaptability, Dr. Black is the esteemed leader you should contact.

Please consider leaving a review of this book on the site where you purchased it. Reviews are the most effective tool in spreading the word to others in need of the information contained in this book.

Thank you for your support!

CONTENTMENT
A Journey of Healing

Dr. Larry D. Black

RESOURCES

American Cancer Society   www. cancer.org

Cancer Research UK: Website   www.cancerresearchuk.org

National Cancer Institute (NCI): www. cancer.gov

Susan G. Komen for the Cure: www.komen.org

St. Jude Children's Research Hospital: www.stjude.org

Made in the USA
Columbia, SC
29 March 2024

33222466R00170